CHALFORD
Oral History
SERIES

voices of
SAFFRON WALDEN
AND SURROUNDING VILLAGES

Saffron Walden Corn Exchange, late 1940s – where it all happened!

CHALFORD
Oral History
SERIES

voices of
SAFFRON WALDEN
AND SURROUNDING VILLAGES

Compiled by
Jean Gumbrell

CHALFORD

The Chalford Publishing Company
St Mary's Mill, Chalford,
Stroud, Gloucestershire, GL6 8NX

ISBN 0 7524 1116 0

Typesetting and origination by
The Chalford Publishing Company
Printed in Great Britain by
Bailey Print, Dursley, Gloucestershire

Haystacks in the snow on the farm facing the Common in Ashdon Road, late 1940s.

CONTENTS

The tuck shop opposite the Boys' British School, 1950s.

INTRODUCTION

I can say, with complete honesty, that collecting the material for this book has been a true labour of love. Listening to all those who have allowed me to interview them in the past and more recently has been both fascinating and instructive. With their words they have painted a picture of a way of life which

Raynhams' Garage at the top of the High Street in the 1920s. The old brewery has now been demolished to make way for houses.

has now gone forever. It was a way of life in a tight-knit agricultural community, when both town and village needed and depended upon one another.

It is all too easy to yearn for the 'good old days' when the pace of life was slower and less complex than today. But all too often 'the good old days' were, in fact, 'the bad old days'. If one is poor, life is never easy, but to be poor in the early decades of the twentieth century was to experience real hardship. And that is what many of the contributors to this book have experienced – real hardship and grinding poverty.

But one thread is clearly woven throughout this miscellany of memories: people never felt sorry for themselves!

Life was too hard and time too short for self-pity. Work had to be done, and the hours might be long, but families had to be fed and clothed and there was no time to bemoan one's fate. Perhaps that is why people seemed happier and more content in the old days.

Poverty and hardship apart, so much has changed in and around Saffron Walden since the beginning of the twentieth century. Farming methods, travel, shopping, medicine and family life in general have all played their part in bringing about a social revolution. Here again, through the words of the people who have experienced these changes, the reader is able to trace the changing pattern in the life of an agricultural community.

A fair on Saffron Walden Common, 1929.

ACKNOWLEDGEMENTS

The author wishes to express her gratitude to all those who have contributed towards this book by recounting their various memories and lending photographs from their personal collections. She would also like to thank the *Cambridge Evening News* and local photographer David Campbell for permission to reproduce various other photographs, Saffron Walden Museum for permission to copy the early photograph of Artisan's Dwellings and Saffron Walden Town Library for permission to copy old advertisements from local almanacs. Lastly and certainly not least, she would like to thank her husband, Michael Gumbrell, for all his support, time and trouble in copying many of the photographs.

Home and family

Emson Tanner's wholesale grocery warehouse in Saffron Walden Market Place, 1920s.

Emma Swan drawing water from the village pump, Hadstock churchyard.

The Market Place

I was born over Emson Tanner's in the Market Place and that is where I grew up. I lived there until I was sixteen and then we moved to Ashdon Road. Everything that went on used to happen in the Market Place. One of my most vivid memories is of the Town Band playing beneath our windows.

Joan Butcher

An Elsan in the Garden

I have lived in this cottage all my life. There were four of us children, three boys and a girl. I am the oldest. The cottage is two up and two down and during my childhood there was no electricity, no water – we got our water from the village pump in the churchyard. All the water had to be carried in a bucket. The lavatory was an old Elsan in the garden. But we were happy. We were not very well off but we always had a decent home, decent bed and good food. Dad always grew most of our food. I have learnt all I know about gardening from my father, and now I grow all my own vegetables.

Albert Rowlandson (Hadstock)

Pork and Rabbit

There were twelve children in our family, six boys and six girls, and I was my parents' fourth child. When I was a few years old we moved to Rock Cottage. It didn't have any running water laid on – we used to drink the water from the river.

I was brought up on pork and rabbit. My father used to keep a pig – he kept two a year – and he used to go out and shoot rabbits. People say you mustn't eat too much fat, but I can't eat a bit of meat without a bit of fat on it. Mother used to melt the pig fat down and put it in pots, and she used to make brawn – I have never tasted brawn like it – it was lovely. My father used to kill two pigs a year. They would salt it down and put it in big earthenware pots called pork pots. Then they would take it out and put it in water overnight to get the salt out of it.

Fred Goodwin (Ashdon)

Cottages

Father was a carpenter and joiner and worked for Joseph Custerson for many years. He was a very skilled man and we had many lovely pieces in our home which father had made.

I'm not sure which year it was, sometime in the late 1920s I think, that numbers 15, 17 and 19 Debden Road were up for sale. I remember my parents discussing the property, because father was always very fond of the cottages, because he had been born there. So he went to the auction and bought all of them for £500.

In those days Debden Road was not considered a very posh address, and opposite our house was a row of cottages known as Hockley Yard which, by today's standards, would be called slums. But some wonderful characters lived in Hockley Yard, people like the Whisken family and the Claydens. My mother, who was extremely kind, would take a hot dinner over to any woman in Hockley Yard who had just had a baby or who was ill. Many times she would be asked to sit up at night with someone who was sick. Later, Hockley Yard was demolished and its inhabitants re-housed in Hollyhock Road, and we all missed them very much when they moved away.

Margaret Warner

Imogen Mollet.

Technically a Cockney

I was born in Crown House which my parents bought in 1917. My parents were very much involved in local government; my mother was chairman of Saffron Walden Rural District Council.

My father, who was technically a cockney, trained as a barrister and practised until the First World War and then he went to work at the Ministry of Munitions under Winston Churchill and got the MBE. By that time he was married, but he didn't like being a barrister so he became a poultry farmer. He was a very good poultry farmer and he had masses of hen houses on the Rider Field next to the Grammar

Artisan's Dwellings early this century.

School. They were all free range but by the end of the Second World War it was not commercially viable.

Imogen Mollet (Newport)

Washing in the Kitchen

My parents were Cecil and Edith Bacon. My father was a bricklayer for Audley End Estate. There were five of us children altogether: Eric, Cyril, Herbert, Winifred and me. The cottage where I was born in Audley End Village was two up and two down with no modern conveniences. The lavatory was outside and we had no bathroom; we had a little kitchen where we washed ourselves. And the houses were lit by oil lamps. They modernized the cottages about thirty-four years ago.

Kate Clark

Artisan's Dwellings

Number 1 Artisan's Dwellings was where I was born in 1924. Later we moved down to No. 15 which looked exactly the same as No. 1 but actually had three bedrooms. Number 1 only had two and there were four children in the family, two boys and two girls. I was a middle child and I had an older brother and two younger sisters.

Vert's Nurseries were on the other side of Artisan's Dwellings and we used to enjoy breaking the panes of glass in their greenhouses. Sometimes we would play cricket in the lane between the two rows of cottages.

Jim Day

Stables

We moved from Thundersley Hall Cottages in Wimbish to Pleasant

Debden Road Service Station, early 1950s.

Valley in 1915 when father was called up for the war. First of all we lived down the road, and then when father came out of the army we came here because where Debden Road Service Station is now, there were stables. Father was a farm worker; he worked on the land with the horses for a large part of his life. This house went with the stables, and then the stables were sold so we went to live in St John's Close, which in those days was 33 Pleasant Valley, and then in 1939 we came back here because the people who lived here died and we were promised this cottage.

Ellen Banks

The Best Room

Number 14 Alpha Place had two staircases and it was three storeys high. It had a front room which mother called our 'best room' and kept locked most of the time. We only used it when we had visitors.

I was allowed in there because I was learning the piano and I would go in there to practise – I was very privileged! It was nicely furnished and mother didn't want us children to spoil it. But we always went in there on Sundays.

Ivy Brown

Making Bricks

I was born in Audley End Village in 1917. There were five boys and three girls in our family. My father worked on the Audley End Estate in Lord Braybrooke's time. This would be about the 1920s. In the beginning he used to work in the brick kiln making bricks and then he eventually went to work in the forest as a forester. They treated their employees quite well.

The Braybrookes were a very nice

13

Audley End Village, 1900.

family. It was such a small community everyone knew everyone else. We used to have outings when we were young. I enjoyed living there.

Henry Bacon

Freedom

We came to Landscape View when I was two or three years old. My mother was a war widow of the First World War. We had been living in Church Street and we moved here because these houses were built for ex-servicemen and ex-servicemen's widows. When we first moved here there was nothing over the road, just fields. And at the bottom of Landscape View, nearer to the town, there was nothing but allotments. It was lovely for us children, we would wander all around the fields.

We had so much freedom, something children don't have these days.

We used to play on the haystacks and we would go into the woods in the autumn and pick nuts and blackberries.

Just beyond Seven Devils Lane there is a wood called Burnt Woman's Plantation. We used to called it 'Bump Woman's Wood', and we used to go there to pick violets and bluebells.

Kath Ellis

Boyhood Days

It was lovely at Audley End Village. I wouldn't swap my boyhood days for anything. My father's brother worked for the Estate and that is how we got a cottage there. We lived in an Estate house. It was a very close-knit village but because my father didn't work on the Estate I was never invited to any of the parties at the Big House like the other children, and I did feel very envious.

Cyril Swan

Sparrow Pie

Wills Ayley Cottages at the bottom of Fox Lane, Sewards End, was where I was born in October 1916. My father worked at Wills Ayley Farm for Mr Hatton. He didn't have any special job on the farm, but he thatched corn-stacks and did all sorts of odd jobs. He was also a carpenter. Previously to that he had worked in Saffron Walden at the Cement Works in Thaxted Road.

There were nine children in our family, and my mother brought up several foundling children as well. I think she fostered about four altogether. Life was pretty hard for us because my father had worked at the Cement Works and all the clay was dug out by hand and he had an accident up there. He also had an ulcerated stomach and the two didn't go together. He was in very poor health.

We were mostly self-supporting. We grew all our own vegetables and caught rabbits and hares, and sometimes we had sparrow pie. I can never remember having sparrow pie, but I was told we did have it from time to time.

My mother used to take in washing. We had a donkey cart and we fetched and delivered the washing. And I can remember we used to fetch the flour, a sack at a time, from the mill at Great Chesterford in the donkey cart. Everyone made their own bread in those

Henry Moore wearing his first 'proper suit', with his sisters, Bessie (centre) and Daisy (right).

days.

One job that children did a lot was picking up stones off the fields and singling out the mangels and turnips. Sugar beet wasn't grown around here until a few years ago. Another thing we used to do was pick up acorns, because there were lots of oak trees around here then.

Henry Moore (Ashdon)

The Foster Child

I was brought up in Sewards End at Elms Farm. My mother died when I was very young and the family was split

15

Edgar Moss at the age of seventeen.

up. Mr and Mrs Giblin who farmed
Elms Farm fostered me. I was always
very happy with the Giblins and looked
on them as my father and mother.

Harold Martin

A Country Boy

I was born at Butler's Farm, Ashdon, in
1926. It was my grandfather's farm. He
was called Mr Everett but I always
called him 'Governor' – I can't
remember what his Christian name was.

I'm glad I was a country boy. I didn't
want to be anything else. I think our
childhood was happy – we had lots of
freedom. We would go into the harvest
fields and our parents never worried

about us. Nothing really went wrong.

Edgar Moss (Ashdon)

Countrified

This cottage was originally one of
three; father knocked two into one
and the third was demolished to make
way for St John's Close. In those days
we had an outside toilet and at the back
it used to be one big yard. That was
where father had his stables and kept
pigs. He used to have two horses. He
was a haulage contractor. His name was
Arthur Tredgett. He started with horses
and carts and then he bought his first
lorry in 1935.

I remember Pleasant Valley as being
very countrified. There were allotments
all along the back as far as Hilltop Lane.

Vi Grimshaw

Snuffy

There were thirteen of us in the
family, nine brothers and three
sisters – and one died at birth. My
father was a tinsmith. He worked at
Dominic's in King Street. He always
wore a bowler hat. It was the first thing
he put on in the morning and the last
thing he took off at night. I never did
know why they called him Snuffy. He
was a very tiny man and he only took
size four in shoes.

Nearly all the people who lived in
Debden Road in those days were
working people and they all had
nicknames. All my brothers had
nicknames. George was the eldest, he

Arthur Tredgett with Tom, 1950.

was called Sonny. Charles was a twin, his name was Barger and Thomas the other twin was called Mata. Ernest was called Doona, James was Jum, Andrew was Porky, Bertram was Ringy and I was called Tramp.

I was called Tramp, I think, because one day I went to my uncle's to take him something and as he heard me, he shouted out, 'Who's that at the door?' and I replied, 'It's only a tramp!'. In those days we had quite a lot of tramps in the area.

Ralph Porter

Puffs

As children we used to go up to grandmother's on Saturday mornings when she was baking. She used to make 'puffs', triangles of a dough-like substance, a bit like bread, but sweeter. She would give them to us still warm from the oven, split and spread with butter.

Richard Faircloth

Mud Houses

I was born in the Mud Houses. They were built by Bells. I really don't know why they called them that, but that is what they were called for a long time. My parents bought the house. They were very comfortable with lovely long gardens and a right of way near the Slade. We used to play in the wood yard at Faircloths' Prairie and the wood yard on the corner, and in the copse in Victoria Gardens. There were very few houses built there then. We used to play whip and top in the road.

Hazel Martin

Family life

About two months after I was born we moved to 94 Debden Road where my parents lived for the next forty years. It was a big detached house with a very big garden. It had both a drawing room and a dining room as well as a large hall and a big kitchen and scullery with a walk-in pantry. (Actually the drawing room was our playroom and the dining room, although it had the big table in it, also had easy chairs around the fire, and was really used as the living room.) Upstairs there were two large bedrooms and two smaller ones and a bathroom. I think the house would have been built about 1900. The best part of the house was the bathroom because it

Margaret, Dick, Jean and Mollie Palmer walking in King Street, early 1930s. Mrs Palmer is behind, with Mr Chilton standing in his shop doorway.

Mr William Gray Palmer's Gentlemen's Outfitters in the High Street.

had a big hot water tank in it. That was the warmest place in the house because there was no central heating and it was my favourite thing to go in there with a book. There were two big rooms up in the attic which were used as storage places.

I am the eldest of four children, three girls and one boy. Mollie was born one year after me and then my brother Dick and then my sister Jean. My father – William Gray Palmer – had the gentlemen's outfitters in the High Street.

From the very beginning I can remember we had one maid called Dolly

Mr Dick Palmer outside his shop in the High Street, 1980s.

who worked as a general maid. And then I remember Gladys, who must only have been fourteen. Gladys came mainly to look after us children. Dolly and mother did all the housework together and it was absolutely all routine. Every job had a special day and each week was exactly the same.

Monday was washing day, and that took pretty well all day. We had a copper in the shed outside and the fire under it had to be lit first thing on Monday morning, and then the clothes were boiled, then rinsed. We had a large bath of blue water which stood outside and all the whites were put in, then everything went through the mangle wet and hung out on the line. I can never really remember any wet Mondays! In the evening all the sheets and anything similar were all shaken and folded and then they were put through the mangle. The sheets were never ironed!

Tuesday the dining room was turned out. It was completely cleaned, all the chairs taken out and the walls dusted down with the cobweb brush. Wednesday two of the bedrooms were done, and Thursday the two smaller bedrooms, plus the hall and stairs and probably the bathroom. Friday the kitchen and scullery got done. Saturday – so far as I know Dolly was there – was mother's main baking day. Dolly didn't help with the baking.

We always had a roast dinner midday on Saturday. All our main meals were midday – at one o'clock – because the shop closed every day from one until two. The meals followed a strict routine too.

19

Jim Surrey with parents Jessie and Alfred Surrey, 1950s.

Sunday we had a cold dinner because it had to be easy. We didn't go to church. Monday was a cold dinner also because it was washing day. Tuesday, the remains of the roast were either minced or stewed and Wednesday was fish; the fishmonger brought the fish first thing in the morning. Thursday was the one day we might have different meals. Very often it was liver and bacon, could have been a stew or sausages. Friday it was always steak and kidney pudding, occasionally steak and kidney pie.

The shop hours were from nine until one and two until six four days of the week. Thursday was half day so father was at home on Thursday afternoon. Saturday of course the shop did not close until nine o'clock at night. Whether it closed at eight I don't know, perhaps father went to the pub for a drink with the staff, anyway it would have been pretty late when he got home on Saturday night. We never saw him.

Weekdays Gladys would arrive about nine o'clock in the morning and take us for a walk (Mollie and me) and we invariably went down to the Mansion at Audley End, and then Dick joined us when he got a bit older.

Both maids stayed for dinner and then after dinner mother took the pram with the two youngest into the town and Gladys took Mollie and me for another walk and quite often it might have been to her mother's house not very far away.

Margaret McGowan

Oil Lamps

When my parents went to live at No. 15 Debden Road in the 1920s it had oil lamps and it was my dad who got the gas company to install gas – this would have been in the 1930s. We

20

were the first to have the gas company to install it in Debden Road and the first to have piped water inside. In those days – as late as the 1950s – the four cottages belonged to one landlord and there was one outside central tap for the four cottages. There was an outside loo and an outside wash-house.

It was my eldest brother, Roy, who installed electricity in the cottage. When he left school he first went to work for the Electricity Board.

John Maddams

Butter or Jam

My mother had nine children but one died. I am the youngest boy. She was a war widow in the First War and she had three children, then she married my father, Alfred Surrey, who was a farm worker. I was born at Cole End Farm, Sewards End, in 1924. Later we moved to Royston, then back to Sewards End and then to Shire Hill Farm. My father was horse-keeper to Mr Gustave Engelmann, and we lived in the farmhouse at Shire Hill. Mr Engelmann was a very kind man and he worked hard. I used to go around the farm and see Mr Engelmann walking about the farm sometimes looking a bit angry. He worked everyone hard but he looked after the men.

My father only got 28s a week and mother had to clothe everyone and put shoes on our feet. She managed to do that and she kept us all clean. She would get the copper on the go and we would get into the old tin bath and have a good scrub down. There was no hot water laid on like they have today.

In those days mother couldn't afford butter and jam on our bread. She would say, 'if you have jam you don't have butter – you have bread and jam!'

Jim Surrey

Money to Spend

The only time there was any money to spend was the bonus after the harvest. Then we had new clothes. It was a good job my father had three daughters and we all learned needlework.

Betty Dennison (Wicken Bonhunt)

Pocket Money

Every week, before the war, we got 3d a week pocket money. With my 3d I would spend 2d on a 2oz bar of Cadbury's chocolate. Cadbury's chocolate in those days had eight little squares, and I would have one a day from Monday to Saturday and then on Sunday, I had two squares. So far as I know I kept to it.

Margaret McGowan

The Common

Vine Lodge, Common Hill, where I was born, was our family home and our first establishment in the town, and it was very soon after my birth that we moved to The Priory – draughty and cold as Hades was hot – nevertheless a lovely enjoyable old place and of course

Percy and Florence Welch's Golden Wedding photo taken in the garden of The Priory, April 1947. Percy and Florence are in the front row, with Captain John Welch in the second row at the extreme right.

ideally situated. The common was naturally our favourite recreation area, and it was handy too for our parents to keep an eye on their children. It was my home until my marriage in 1949.

My grandfather, Percy John Welch, was the only veterinary surgeon in the Saffron Walden area, and he was assisted by my father who did not have any formal training.

Captain C.J. Welch

Transport

I can remember riding in a pony and trap with Mr Goodwin. He was the chimney sweep here and he was also Church Warden and we went to Royston in his trap. We used to have one bus on Tuesday to go to Walden and a trip to Saffron Walden was really something. We didn't go there often. Everyone walked everywhere. The vicar was the only person with a car – it had a 'dickey seat' at the back.

Betty Dennison (Wicken Bonhunt)

Key in the Flower Pot

I lived in the bungalow almost opposite Goldstones in Ashdon. My father was Walter Lawrence and he called the bungalow 'Fruit Farm'. He used to grow the most wonderful strawberries. Whenever my mother went to Saffron Walden on her bike, it was the only

Bridget Ennis (née Lawrence) in Brownie uniform at the extreme right, playing in the garden of her home in Ashdon with Pat Witty (née Furze), left, and a friend.

time she would lock the door, and leave a note on it saying 'key in flower pot' with an arrow pointing towards the flower pot.

Bridget Ennis (Ashdon)

She Hated Eggs

My father was Mr Charles Beadle's gamekeeper and my grandfather was his farm manager. He lived in Chardwell Farmhouse and my parents lived at Fosters Farm Cottages, Arkesden. My grandmother used to keep chickens and wash the eggs every week for market. She said she hated eggs! She never would eat them.

When Mr Beadle died his farms were bought up by different people and Chardwell was bought by Mr Cowell who lived in Fairycroft House in Saffron Walden. He had a chauffeur, Mr Paul Priest, who had a wooden leg, and my grandmother, who used to make a lot of home-made wine, would give him a glass whenever he called at the cottage.

Irene Hudgell (Arkesden)

As Clear as Crystal

We moved to Sewards End when I was six and lived at Wheel Hall Cottages, now called Wheel Hall. We didn't have running water but drew the water from a spring and it was as clear as crystal. We used to go across the fields

23

with a yoke and two buckets. It was lovely water.

We used to go out and leave the doors open and leave the gypsies in charge. My father used to lend one of them money and take his watch in return. Then it might be two years later, the gypsy would return the money and my father would say, 'Here you are Bill – here's your watch!'

Sylvia Richardson

The Bean Pod

My parents, William and Annie Thake, had been married ten months when I was born and, although they didn't know it, I was to be their only child. I was born at The Bean Pod, Howe Lane, Great Sampford in 1932. I've never been sure why it was called The Bean Pod, but my father always said that he thought it had been a public house, or perhaps a beer house, at one time. I remember we had a large outhouse with a big stone sink with storage space above, which might have been used as a brew house.

My father was a farmworker at Radwinter Hall. His boss, Mr Portway, owned Radwinter Threshers Ltd and rented out traction engines and men to the farmers round about, and my father drove one of the traction engines.

Father always took his midday meal with him, and one of my earliest memories is of my mother getting father's food ready and putting it into a snow-white linen drawstring bag kept especially for the purpose. She was a lovely cook. Although the meals we had were plain, they were very nourishing and beautifully cooked. She'd been born in London and was in service there before she married my father. Although we didn't have much money, and by today's standards The Bean Pod was very primitive, mother made the whole place very comfortable and cheerful – not an easy task with no running water and an outside lavatory with a bucket. (After a time this bucket would wear thin and be replaced by a new one. The old bucket could then be seen upside down in the garden to draw early spring rhubarb.)

We got our drinking water from a standing tank a few yards from the house. This tank was filled by the Council about twice a week. For washing clothes and floors there was a pond in our front garden which was always covered with slimy green duckweed. We had no electricity, just oil lamps downstairs and candles for the bedrooms. For cooking, mother had an old-fashioned open-bar range and an oil stove with two burners and an oven which stood on top.

The kitchen was lovely and roomy with a scrubbed brick floor, two rush mats in the centre and a scrubbed wooden table which, on special occasions when we had visitors, was covered with American cloth to make it look grander.

Margaret Rust (Radwinter)

Young Stanley Wilson, an ardent socialist, holding forth in Saffron Walden Market Place, late 1920s.

The Gentry and Others

I was born at No. 1 Artisan's Dwellings in 1924. My parents lived there soon after they married. As children we used to run along the flat roofs.

When we were children it was very much the gentry and others. Stanley Wilson was the biggest shock to Walden when he grew up!

Joy Waterman

Livestock

There was a lovely old couple, Mr and Mrs Farrow. He used to have a pigsty at the bottom of the garden and keep half a dozen pigs in it. He would fatten them up and then drive them out of the front gate and drive them down to market. And I have often seen a load of cows going down the road being driven to market.

In those days everyone in Pleasant Valley used to keep half a dozen chickens down at the bottom of the garden. I used to keep Belgium Hare rabbits. When they were about six or seven weeks old I used to take them to the market. The dealers used to come down from London and buy them because they were so tender, then they would sell them off as chicken. A lot of people bred rabbits for food in those days.

Johnny Porter

Charles Henry Underwood outside his blacksmith's shop in Radwinter at the turn of the century.

Blacksmith

My grandfather was the village blacksmith but my father had a smallholding. My grandfather and my great-grandfather lived here – I think the Underwood family have lived in this cottage for about two hundred years. My grandfather's name was Charles Underwood. Originally the family came from Steeple Bumpstead.

I was born at Prince's Well. This was the blacksmith's shop until we were married in 1937 and we came to live here then. The cottage goes back to 1450 and we still have the medieval doorways. It is an old Essex hall house. There is a mummified cat which tumbled out of the chimney breast in 1982. The chimney was dated 1628.

Joyce Jarvis (Radwinter)

Real Smoked Bacon

My parents came to Clock House in 1903 when they were married. My father took a tenancy – in those days Clock House was part of Sir Walter Gilby's Estate. I am the eldest of five children; I had two half brothers and two half sisters.

In the early days Clock House Estate was not very big – about 54 acres. It was a small mixed farm and in 1936 father hired The White House which had 70 acres so it made it bigger. My two brothers and myself were always expected to help on the farm.

We were mostly self-supporting. We kept pigs and every now and again someone would come in to kill one of them. It would be hung from two iron rings in the beam above our heads. Then we would soak one of the legs in brine and herbs and after a while take it down the road to an old lady called Mrs. Fitch.

She would hang the leg in her big inglenook fireplace and after a while we would collect it. The muslin which covered it would be black with soot but inside it was real smoked bacon. Not like the stuff you get now. It was lovely!

Fred Brook (Little Sampford)

Meat Pudding

I can remember my grandfather used to work in the fields and my granny used to make him a meat pudding in a basin and tie it up from corner to corner in a red handkerchief, and we would take it out to the fields to him.

Mollie Moore (Ashdon)

Wellknown Bee Keeper

My father bought this house for £75 in 1920. It was two farm cottages which he made into one. I was born here in 1922 and I have lived here all my life. Father was one of ten children and he was born in Hempstead but came to Great Sampford to work at Calthorpes and ended up farming it himself. He married a Scottish lady called Amy who was a war widow from the First War. They met when she came to stay with her sister who was married to the local miller, Mr Wisby.

My father was a well known bee keeper and he had quite a few hives and he sold his honey which helped him to set up on his own. He was actually in partnership with his brother Ralph who

Bill and Daphne Reader outside their cottage, bought by Bill's father in 1920 for £75.

was killed in the First War two weeks before the Armistice.

Bill Reader (Great Sampford)

Idyllic

We came to Orford House about 1908. It was lovely. It was a beautiful house and we had a most tremendously happy home. It was simply marvellous, that is why I was not happy at school. I was educated at boarding school and I hated it. Then I was sent to Paris because I had already started to sing.

My parents entertained quite a lot

27

Orford House, Ugley.

Mr William Reader of Great Sampford, a well-known beekeeper.

and we used to have a lot of people staying in the house. We used to play a lot of tennis.

People loved my parents. When they celebrated their golden wedding the whole village came in the afternoon and we danced Sir Roger de Coverly on the lawn. We were never at all grand. We were not a County Family at all, but we had masses of friends. Sometimes there were eighteen of us at weekends. We used to have lovely dances in the drawing room. We had a dance every year right up until we left in 1950. It was idyllic.

The Tennants were a firm of metal merchants but my father was very interested in farming. When he retired he was very busy at Orford House with a pedigree herd. I think there were about 75 acres in those days.

Miss Nancy Tennant (Ugley)

CHAPTER 2

Schooldays

South Road School having a nature lesson on Shire Hill, 1920. Ivy Brown (née Barber) is at the extreme right talking to her teacher, Miss Masters.

Great Chesterford at the turn of the century.

A Stupid Idea

I was an only child and my mother insisted that I went to a private school, and I went to one in Audley Road. It was an all girls' school and there were only about twenty of us in all. Personally now, I think it was a rather stupid idea.

Joan Butcher

Path

I went to Great Chesterford School. We walked there every day along the same path as Mr Emson's cows, which made life very difficult during wet weather. Our mothers would take it in turns to carry us across that part of the path used by the cows.

I left school at fourteen, but I had got as far as I could long before that and I was usually put to doing the gardening in the school. Once after the pea-pickers had been during the pea harvest, there were patches of peas in the field which were unripe. When they were ready for picking, the farmer asked me if I would like to pick them, but I was caught and hauled over the coals for playing truant and sent back to school, where I was sent out into the garden to do some gardening!

Eddie Clayden (Little Chesterford)

Ethel

I went to the village school and I loved it. We used to play games on the village green. The school has now been

30

pulled down and the land is the lawn of a private house.

Miss Penn, the headmistress, was very strict but she was a very good teacher. She taught me a lot, including how to use a sewing machine, and before I had left school I was helping her to make loose covers because she was moving into a cottage in the village. She taught me sewing and it has stood me in good stead. I love needlework. I used to make my own dresses when I was single and I had a dummy I called Ethel.

Irene Hudgell (Arkesden)

The Miss Gowletts

When I was six years old we – my two sisters, my brother and myself – went to Cambridge House School which was run by the Miss Gowletts, and we were still there when it moved to Chaters Hill in the 1930s.

I remember the Miss Gowletts as very

Eddie Clayden.

Cambridge House School

Is an old-established Private Boarding and Day School for Girls, conducted upon the best High School principles. The School Buildings are modern ; the Class-rooms large, airy and well-equipped. A garden and playground are attached to the house, and a large Playing Field is situated at a short distance from the School. Pupils are prepared for various examinations— London Matriculation, Cambridge Locals, Diocesan Examination in Religious Knowledge, Associated Board of Music, and the Royal Drawing Society .

Advert for Cambridge House School, 1933.

Mrs Norrie Kemp on the back row at the extreme left, with some of her pupils at Ashdon School shortly before she retired.

old ladies, especially Miss Alice who did most of the teaching. Miss Annie did drawing and painting and Miss Hannah was the housekeeper. There was a Miss Cecil who used to take the youngest class and Miss Woolf came in to play the piano for dancing.

We used to go home for lunch and one day we stayed. We went into the dining room and my sister, Mollie, promptly sat down and was promptly told to stand up because Grace had not been said. I sat down and was told to move down one place and I tried to slide from chair to chair and fell over.

Miss Annie took us for painting and for games and we went down to Abbey Lane where the council flats are now. Years ago they were playing fields and they had tennis down there. We had our games and Miss Annie had painting

down there in the Pavilion. In those days we were taught copper-plate writing. I don't remember doing arithmetic – perhaps just adding-up sums. We were never afraid of the Miss Gowletts.

Then we all four left Cambridge House and went to the Friends' School. This would be January 1936 and soon after that Cambridge House closed because the number of pupils had been dwindling and it must have been a blow when all four of us left at once. We went to the Junior House school at the Friends' but I only had two terms there before I went into the Big School. I really enjoyed school just so long as I could play games.

Margaret McGowan

The Schoolhouse

My husband was appointed head of Ashdon School in 1950 and stayed until he retired in 1973. We lived in the Schoolhouse. There was no sanitation, only Rose Cottage at the bottom of the garden. No bathroom, but in the kitchen there was a sink and a bath with an enormous wooden lid which had to be lifted up and hooked up on to the wall. Then you had to pour in hot water. But at least you could pull the plug out and the water ran away. For the first few years there was a kitchen range, and then we had that removed and a Rayburn put in which heated the hot water system.

Norrie Kemp

Depopulated

I came to Saffron Walden because I was head of a village school in Suffolk and the area was becoming depopulated. I came to the Boys' British as a teacher. When Mr Heaven retired and Mr Elsden became head I then became senior assistant.

The Boys' British did not have a playground so we used the 14 acres of the common as our playground and each class had its own football pitch. Part of Friday afternoon was given up to football or cricket and the male members of the staff joined in.

Tom Dewing

School photo of Dorothy Bartlett (née Cardy), 1930s.

One of the Rougher Lads

I was a young tinker at school. I was one of the rougher lads. We would play the teachers up a bit. I had quite a lot of caning when I went to school but I don't think it has done me any harm.

Jim Surrey

The Watch

One thing I remember was a rag and bone man who came to the school at lunch times. If you took a bag of rags he would give you a present. If you took a big bag of rags, the present was a

33

Sewards End School early this century.

watch. As I lived at Water End I never went home at lunch time but one day I discovered that the rag and bone man was coming that very lunch time, and I badly wanted a watch. So I walked all the way back from school in my lunch hour and gave my mother such a shock when I arrived home. I explained what had happened and asked her for a big bag of rags. She found some and I walked all the way back to school, only to find that the rag and bone man had been and gone!

When I eventually started work, the first thing I did was to save up for a watch!

Dorothy Bartlett (Ashdon)

A Bit of a Rebel

My first school was Cambridge House School. This was in the Miss Gowletts' time and I can remember standing in a corner with a dunce's hat on my head for some misdemeanour. Then I went to the Friends' School for a spell. But I was a bit of a rebel and I was asked politely to leave, which did not go down very well with my father because he'd been a teacher there for several years.

Nona Dawkins

Hot Drinks

My first day at Sewards End school there was deep snow and my brother and sister had to help me through the big drifts. There was a lovely teacher called Miss Green. She was a wonderful headmistress and ever so kind to the children. We used to take potatoes to school and cut our initials on them and then the teacher put them in a big fire in the school for our dinner. We also took cocoa and sugar and Miss Green boiled milk so we could have a hot drink at midday.

It was a small school with a big bell on top and the boys used to shoot stones at it with their catapults to make the bell ring.

Jim Surrey

A Young Farmers' Club

I really enjoyed my school days. We had a Young Farmers' Club and we did bee keeping and we also had a plot of garden and did gardening. We had social events and outings. My schooldays were very happy. I got my scholarship when I was fourteen and I went to what was then known as Cambridge Technical School. I did nursery training, which came in very useful when I had my four children, but I never became a nursery nurse.

Dorothy Bartlett (Ashdon)

The School Bus

I remember going to Dame Bradbury's School on a Wiffen's bus. We were dropped off at the gas works and we would walk up Chaters Hill. All the local buses from all the villages used to park on the Common. Once I mislaid my bus money and I hid between some very large ladies at the back of the bus to avoid detection.

Another time I played truant from school with my sister. My sister had saved her pocket money and we went for an ice cream at the Copper Kettle in King Street and then we had to sit around all day to catch the bus on the way home.

Sometimes I would see Dr George Gray driving his Rolls around the town. I went to school with the Gray children and the Edgars and Dr Patterson's children. When he retired I took over his practice. Once I deliberately missed the school bus on the way home so that I could go and ask uncle George Gray for a lift home in his Rolls Royce.

Dr John Eaton

Punished

I went to the village school all the time. I remember when the evacuees came down – there were so many of us in school – the village boys and girls went in the morning one week and the evacuees in the afternoon, then the next week we swapped over. The headmaster's name was Mr Enoch. He was very strict – he punished us for the least little thing.

Edgar Moss (Ashdon)

Heart of Gold

Mr Heaven was headmaster at the Boys' British. He was a little man

Boys' British sports team, 1932.

with a big moustache. He was very strict. If you could not learn he would try to knock it into you. He wore a big gold ring and if you didn't grasp what he was telling you he would clip you around the head – and that ring hurt!

But he had a heart of gold. He was a very kind man. One day, it was during the dinner hour and he asked me if I had any dinner and when I said no, he went into the house and his wife made me some jam sandwiches. I can taste that jam now. It tasted lovely!

Jim Surrey

Tommy Bag

At first I went to Sewards End school and then when I was nine I went to the Boys' British. I had to walk there from Sewards End and used to take my lunch in my 'Tommy bag' – a canvas bag with a drawstring. We took sandwiches and perhaps a hard boiled egg, which was usually squashed to pieces when we fought because we would throw our hard boiled eggs at each other.

Harold Martin

Boots with Studs

We did have a small school but it was closed by the time I reached school age. I had to go to Arkesden school. We walked all the way and we wore boots with studs in them. We used to see how many studs we could kick out before we got home.

Betty Dennison (Wicken Bonhunt)

36

Hadstock School, 1926.

A Strict School

My mother-in-law was born in Hadstock and went to Hadstock school. It was a church school, and the headmistress was Miss Salmon and she was also the post mistress. It was a very strict school, under the direction of the Revd W. Smith. The boys and girls had separate playgrounds and there were just two rooms, one for the younger children and one room for the boys and girls. The children left school at the age of thirteen.

Reg Wood (Hadstock)

Tortoise Stove

I went to the village school and left at the age of fourteen. The old school master taught the upper classes and his wife taught the infants. The school was very cold in winter, as it was only heated by an old tortoise stove.

One of the boys in my class at school – Alec Young – used to give us rides in his sugar-box trolley from the top of Wenden Hill to Duck Street River. It was a Tate & Lyle wooden sugar box on four wheels which was started by foot or strings, we didn't need a push once we got started. At playtime we would be visited by his tame jackdaw.

Ron Cain (Wendens Ambo)

Buttons like Saucers

I started at Great Sampford school when I was five years old, after the harvest holidays. It was quite an occasion: my mother took me to a dressmaker in the village for a new coat.

Wendens Ambo School, 1924. Back row, left to right: Charlie Judd, Cecil Richardson, Percy Clark, Bob Clark, George Law, Reg White, Vic Clark, Ron Cain, Albert Reynolds. Next row: Frieda Coe, Frieda Thomas, Molly Law, Lizzie Sibley, Vera Challis, Irene Pluck, Ida Driver, Gladys Richardson, Kathy Freeman, Doris Law, Dora Richardson. Front two rows: Dolly Sibley, Doris Savill, Marjorie Thomas, May King, Ernie Reynolds, Bernard Pluck, George Tickner, Fred Judd, Walter Hartswell.

I can see it now, it was a small brown check with big saucer-like buttons, and I had new brown shoes. The school was about a mile away and when it was fine and dry I could go through the fields by a short cut which brought me quite near to the school.

There were two teachers at Great Sampford School - the headmaster, Mr Blayney, who was Irish and very strict, and Miss Andrews the infants' teacher. She cycled every day from Thaxted on a high bicycle with a dress guard, and a rather large basket in front. We would take it in turns to carry her brown leather bag into school which always seemed full up.

We had to take sandwiches for lunch as school dinners hadn't been thought of then, so mother bought me a small satchel, but often when I went for my sandwiches someone had been helping themselves! So that was stopped, and a kind lady from the village let me go to her home and have my dinner with her daughter, Florrie, who was a few years older than me, but went to the same school.

Margaret Rust (Radwinter)

A Pupil Teacher

I was a pupil teacher at Great Sampford school during the time Mr Blayney was headmaster. He used to scare me stiff but eventually we became very

Radwinter School (with bell tower), 1911.

good friends and I was very friendly with his daughter. Those were the days of the pupil teacher, and one day a week I would cycle to the Training College in Saffron Walden.

Daisy Brook (Little Sampford)

Brown Felt Hat

We moved to Radwinter when I was six and a half because the farmer who owned our cottage wanted to sell it. We'd only been in Radwinter a week when it was decided I should go to school. My mother took me and a little lady came up to us wearing a small apron and a brown felt hat on her head, mother asked if she could see the headmistress and she said, 'I am the headmistress!'

Margaret Rust (Radwinter)

Kept In

I went to South Road school until I was eleven. My father wanted me to help him with his milk round and the headmistress didn't like that at all and used to keep me in deliberately. So I transferred to the National School in Castle Street. (Those were the days when milk was delivered in cans with a measure hanging on the side.)

Molly Porter

All the Teachers were Strict

I went to the Boys' British School. Mr Elsden, the headmaster, was a marvellous teacher, and I used to have Mr Dewing, Mr Tinnion and Mrs Trinder – she was a very good teacher. In those days though, all the teachers were strict.

Johnny Porter

39

Castle Street School, 1931.

Mrs Ludgate's Desk

On Fridays at school we would polish
Mrs Ludgate's desk. We would take
a nice, soft piece of cloth for the polish
and another to rub it off. It was always
Mansion polish we used and we would
take turns and polish away until it
gleamed.

Margaret Rust (Radwinter)

CHAPTER 3

Treats

Castle Street School Coronation party, 1953.

The Town Band

Molly and Ralph Porter used to take their daughter, Audrey, and me every Saturday evening to listen to the Town Band playing in the Market Place. The highlight of the evening being a lovely bag of hazelnut whirls from Nuttalls – now the Golden Butterfly. Simple things like that – listening to the Band in the Market Place – which perhaps today children would think dull – gave us so much pleasure.

Margaret Warner

King and Queen

Mrs Bramwell Jackson used to have a party for the children of Wicken at Christmas. May Day was a big day. We would decorate hoops with flowers and we would have a King and Queen. There was always something to look forward to.

Once the Women's Institute had an outing to the seaside and the bus broke down at Marks Tay, so they had to wait for another and they all started putting their ears to the ground to hear if the charabanc was coming.

Betty Dennison (Wicken Bonhunt)

Nuts

There was a grocers shop at No. 11 Debden Road run by George Bedford. He was quite a jovial man and every First of May he would scramble nuts and sweets on the pavement outside his shop. There was always a fight to see which child collected the most and we were always joined by the children from Castle Street much to our annoyance.

I remember when I first started at Cambridge House School, my mother told me I could not go out into the street to take part in the scramble wearing my school uniform, the Miss Gowletts would not approve. Nevertheless, when the local paper came out the next week, there I was on the front page, fighting away in my school uniform. Needless to say the Miss Gowletts hauled me over the coals for my unladylike behaviour, but it didn't make any difference, I always enjoyed a scramble and a rough and tumble.

Margaret Warner

Horse-drawn Wagonette

The Chapel Sunday School had a treat every year. We used to go in a horse-drawn wagonette to Rickling to Mr Tinney's farm. There we used to have games. Sometimes we went to Clavering.

Irene Hudgell (Arkesden)

May Day

We never did it, but on May Day children would come around to the house with flowers, mostly bluebells, they had collected from the woods and they would be given a penny (no one ever took their flowers).

Margaret McGowan

Wonderful Moments

Christmas in Ashdon started about a fortnight before Christmas, maybe a little bit earlier. We would be coming out of school and one boy – perhaps in a hurry to get home – would reach Crown Hill, then stop and stare at the tiny window. Then he would turn and yell back at us: 'Eason's have got their Christmas things in! Then we would run like the devil to this tiny window, and press our noses against the glass glorying in all the wonderful toys and things on display. They weren't very sophisticated toys, just small dolls (not Barbie), little houses, games, puzzles, lorries and trucks, boxes of biscuits, chocolates and sweets.

All of us would jockey for positions and shout excitedly: I'm going to get my mum to get me that (probably we hadn't a hope in hell of getting it, but it was lovely to dream!). But I remember that my mother did actually buy me a box of biscuits with a picture of Father Christmas's house on the lid. I spent a long time with my nose squashed against it, trying to look through the painted window and going completely cross-eyed in my efforts to see Father Christmas inside the tin!

Bridget Ennis (Ashdon)

Christmas at the Big House

Every Christmas the people who worked on the Audley End Estate were given bread and meat and sometimes clothing. And they always had a party for the village children in the Big Hall. The butler used to wait

Frank Moss, aged 21, a soldier in the Great War who later became Father Christmas.

upon us and everyone had presents. I suppose there are still a few of those presents around today.

Henry Bacon

The Table and the Tree

Mrs Luddington gave a Christmas party for all the children of Ashdon at Waltons Park. We would assemble on Crown Hill, the girls wearing their Sunday dresses and the boys all smart and shiny faced. Then, our teachers, Mrs Eason and Mrs Luff, would escort us to Waltons Park. We would chatter like magpies all the way

Pupils of Ashdon School at Waltons, 1920s.

make ourselves comfortable on the floor, whilst Mrs Luddington took up her position near the table. Then the door would open and in would come Father Christmas (it was really Frank Moss, Edgar's father, the village postman).

When Father Christmas arrived, Mrs Luddington would call out our names, one by one, to come and receive a present. I always marvelled at the way she knew all our names. It never dawned on me until years later that she used the school register! And I truly believed that Mrs Luddington had gone round Saffron Walden market the week previously and chosen a present especially for me. The presents were always so very suitable for the recipients.

When it was time for us to go home, as we put on our coats and said, 'Thank you very much Mrs Luddington', we would be given an orange to send us on our way back to Crown Hill.

Bridget Ennis (Ashdon)

Eason's Window

My aunt, Mrs Eason, used to turn her front room into a little shop and decorate the window with toys and things just for Christmas. We always looked in the window when we came out of school to see what she'd got. They were only small toys, fire-engines and little lorries – that sort of thing – because in those days people could not afford so much.

Edgar Moss (Ashdon)

until reaching our destination and then as we took off our coats we became shy and tongue-tied, speaking only when spoken to.

When we were ready, the inner doors were opened and you could hear the sharp intake of breath as we saw the Table. It was a long trestle table running the length of the room absolutely laden with the most wonderful food! Our shyness was soon forgotten once we had been told to help ourselves.

After we had eaten our fill we were ushered into a beautiful oak-panelled room with a huge log fire crackling in the fireplace, and a beautifully decorated Christmas tree reaching up to the ceiling. There was a table beside the tree laden with parcels. We were told to

44

Salvation Army

Years ago every Sunday the Salvation Army Band played at the junction of Debden Road and London Road, and after they had been round with the collecting bag, they would then march down the High Street to the Citadel in Castle Street – later it became the Snowflake Laundry; now it's all houses.

Ralph Porter

The Special Present

We always got just one present at Christmas – that was our yearly present – and we thought the world of it and really looked after it. Once I got a steam lorry and I idolized it for years; in fact I wish I had it now! We also had a stocking filled with sugar mice, sweets and an orange, and perhaps a bright new penny.

Edgar Moss (Ashdon)

Empire Day

On Empire Day, all the schools used to march to the Common where every child was given an orange and a bun. I think we did wear a little bit of red, white and blue ribbon attached to our lapels with a pin. I don't know who gave us the oranges and buns but there were big trestle tables, one with oranges and one with buns. I think we had a holiday.

Margaret McGowan

A Party at the Aerodrome

A letter arrived at school one morning from the aerodrome at Debden which was occupied by the Americans at that time. They invited all the children up to the age of twelve to a party on Boxing Day. I was twelve but I was able to go. In the afternoon we were waiting in our best clothes and the American truck arrived and we all scrambled into the back for a ride to the aerodrome. When we got there, there was a huge Christmas tree decked out with presents and great big trays of sweets and candy bars. We were told to help ourselves. And there was a marvellous tea rounded off with jelly and ice cream. When we were ready to come home we all had a parcel of candies and chewing gum.

Margaret Rust (Radwinter)

Big Money

Yes, we would go carol singing. If you got a shilling, perhaps two shillings or half a crown, you were really lucky, because that was a lot of money in those days. But you only got that sort of money at the posh houses and you used to have to really sing for that!

Edgar Moss (Ashdon)

Hadstock Mothers' Union outing, 1951. Mrs Renee Wood is on the back row, second from the right.

Hadstock Village outing on Long Lizzie at the turn of the century.

CHAPTER **4**

Working life

Stacking corn at Yews Farm, Hadstock, 1920s. This is now the site of Hadstock Aerodrome. Mr Arthur
Crawley is in the centre foreground with his daughters, Ruth and Hilda.

First-Class DAIRY PRODUCE

PROMPT and COURTEOUS SERVICE

Milk Minus Microbes.

Microbes

When I left school it was harvest time so I went to work for Mr Emson at Manor Farm leading the horses into the field. At the age of eighteen I was used to carrying extremely heavy weights – 18 stones of wheat, 19 stones of beans and 20 stones of clover!

Manor Farm had a dairy herd. It was the first dairy herd to be tuberculin tested locally and it was advertised as 'Milk Minus Microbes'. They sold it to Saffron Walden General Hospital first and then all around Saffron Walden. The cows were British short-horns. There were two milk vans drawn by horses, but around the village it was sold from a wooden barrow.

Eddie Clayden (Little Chesterford)

Cycle Shop

I left the village school when I was fourteen and there was a cycle shop in Saffron Walden called Walbro's and my dad was friendly with the manager. He advertised for a cycle mechanic and I went to see him and he offered me 7s 6d a week, but my father didn't think much of that. My father worked for the Bartlow Estate and so I got a job there for 10s 6d a week. I was a general farm worker. The farm changed hands after eighteen months but I stayed for almost thirteen years. After leaving Bartlow Estate I went to Hall Farm to work for Mr Alan Free. I was there two years and he gave up and so I went to work for Myhills on the aerodrome. It was hard work, we had to carry sacks of grain weighing between 16 and 18 stones.

Albert Rowlandson (Hadstock)

Saffron Walden High Street showing Walbro's to the right of the Abbey Hotel, 1940s.

No Money in Farming

There was no money in farming when I left school. Father bought £1,000 worth of cattle from Cambridge cattle market and had them driven from Cambridge to Hadstock by a drover. He fattened them and took them back to Cambridge and got his £1,000 back and nothing else. The same thing happened with our pigs and sheep. We used to have a lot of sheep and they got foot and mouth disease and every morning we had to catch them and pull the scabs off them and put Stockholm Tar on them – and we never lost a lamb!

By the time I left the farm things were so bad they sold Hadstock Wood, about eleven acres. They sold it because the trees were straight and tall and were the only ones they could find for the roof of a church in Yorkshire. I think Mr Bell of Walden bought them. He came over to Hadstock and he and father counted the trees, then it was a question of 'how much?'. So they each sat down on opposite sides of my father's desk and wrote down a figure – and they both wrote down exactly the same figure – £840 – which was a fortune in those days, and that saved us from going bankrupt. I think father's and uncle's life insurance was also used to save the farm. Farmers were going broke all around.

Ralph Crawley (Hadstock)

Long Lizzie, Yews Farm, Hadstock, at the turn of the century.

Big Heavy Lorries

My father, Charles William Coe, served in the First War and then he joined Emson Tanner as a driver. First of all Emson Tanner had vans and they had fairly big heavy lorries. My father went all around the area and sometimes I used to go with him. He used to start at seven-thirty in the morning and was supposed to finish at six but very often he did not get home until ten o'clock at night.

Joan Butcher

Wooden Plough

I left the village school at the age of fourteen in 1923 and went straight to Hill Farm to Mr Hagger. For my first day's work I had two horses and a wooden plough. There was a man with me and he was earning a man's wages, 25s a week and I was only a boy but we were both doing the same job and I was getting 3s 6d. When I took my first week's wages home I thought I was so big! I gave them to my mother and she gave me 6d back.

I started work at six-thirty in the morning and worked until five o'clock in the evening. We had half an hour for breakfast and then we would work until two o'clock. We had one hour for dinner then in the afternoon we used to do odd jobs until we knocked off. We used to take our breakfast with us. We had bread and cheese and sometimes an onion. We used to have a whole onion peeled with a pen knife in one hand and a piece of bread with a little bit of butter or dripping in the middle of it, and we would take a bite of onion and then a bite of bread. We never used to

The late Fred Goodwin. The meadow he ploughed as a lad in 1923 is in the background.

wash our hands – there was nowhere to wash them.

It was hard work. There was not a job on the farm which I couldn't do. There used to be a dozen corn stacks up at Hill Farm and I used to be able to thatch a stack – we had to – they made you. You just had to do as you were told. But my love was horses. My father was a horse-keeper at Hill Farm, he was up there all his lifetime.

Fred Goodwin (Ashdon)

Only Two Holidays

I left school at fourteen but I was working before that, helping with the harvest and working as houseboy for Mrs Isobel Furze at Goldstones. I used to clean the shoes and cut wood and do the fires.

A boy's first job on the farm was leading the horses and carting the dung from the farmyard out into the field. You went hoeing with the men and they taught you how to do it. You were really apprenticed. You didn't get a man's money until you were twenty-one. So you had seven years before you had a man's pay which was about 30s a week.

It was a fifty-two hour week without weekends when I first started work in 1920. Stockmen and horse-keepers did extra time of course. We used to start work at half past six. Horse-keepers started at half past five. They did an

Henry Moore, working at Ricketts Farm, Ashdon, 1940s.

hour's feeding and grooming the horses which had to be ready by half past six, and they got 1s 6d a week extra for doing that.

We started work at half-past six and worked until five and had no holidays. There wasn't a daily holiday and you had a job to get a Saturday afternoon off at one time. I think we worked until half-past one on Saturday. Before I began working I think they worked a six-day week. We only had two holidays a year – Boxing Day and August Bank Holiday.

Henry Moore (Ashdon)

Sixpence an Hour

I used to go cleaning for sixpence an hour. One job I did was scrubbing the floor of the bar at the Duke of York. But when the County High School opened I went up there as a cleaner and, of course, I got more money. Then I went cleaning the nurses' quarters at the hospital in London Road. I was there from 1969 to 1971 and I loved it, but unfortunately I had to retire because of my age.

Rosie Porter

The Workhouse

I went to South Road Girls' School and when I left school I worked at Stead & Simpsons, the shoe shop in King Street, until the war broke out. Then I had to go to the workhouse in Radwinter Road to do domestic work. I was not very happy there. Seeing all the poor old men who were homeless used to really upset me, and as soon as I could, I left.

Hazel Martin

No Factories

When we left school it was just understood that we went on the farm – there were no factories like there are today. I went to work on my uncles' farm, Reg, Fred and Alf Everett, in partnership with Butlers and Nutts. In those days Nutts Farm was a small thatched cottage; later it was pulled down and a modern bungalow built in its place.

On the farm I did everything a boy was told to do. My grandfather had horses but when I started work tractors were coming in and we had about two horses. I was on the farm for about sixteen years and then I had a bad illness and I had to give up farming so I went to work at the village butcher's shop to work for my uncle Mr Charles Peplow. I worked at the butcher's shop for about fourteen years and during that time the business changed hands and was owned by Mr Banks, but Mr Harold Goodwin was the head assistant at the shop. I owe an awful lot to him – he taught me everything about the butchering trade.

I drove one of the three butcher's vans and we used to go all over the area. The housewife would leave the key for you and you would undo the door and if they hadn't got a fridge you knew just where to put the meat. People trusted you. They would leave a note on the table telling you what they wanted for the weekend. It was the way we lived. They were happy days. Everyone was nice, but the village was the best.

While I was working for the butcher my father was doing the post round and was also caretaker of the village school. When he retired after thirty-two years he asked me if I would like to take the job on. By that time the butcher's business had changed hands so I decided I would become the postman and later I also became the school caretaker. I did the post round for the next twenty-five years and was school caretaker for twenty-two.

Edgar Moss (Ashdon)

Correspondence Course

After I left the Boys' British I served as a joiner in Bishop's Stortford, then I 'shoved around' various places including working in London but came home during the Depression of 1932 to work for my father who was a builder. I still carry on the family business. We never started on a job or finished it without father going to inspect it to see whether it was right or wrong. He always insisted on keeping his eye on things.

I was the one to set up the undertaking side of the business as another branch of the family business. By this time the building side of the business had increased but I had been undertaking for quite a while. Then I did a correspondence course in embalming and went up to Blackburn to do the practical side. I was admitted to the B.I.E. on 24th March 1944. I believe I was the first embalmer in the town.

Richard Faircloth

The George, with the Blacksmith's House in George Street at the extreme right.

A Genuine Blacksmith

My father was a genuine blacksmith. A farrier shoes horses, a blacksmith does metal work; my father did both. My father came to Walden in 1922. We lived in the Smith's House in George Street, now the Oxfam shop.

I was an only boy. I took over the business in 1944 and in 1945 we turned the smithy into an engineering works. A forge is a more appropriate word. The forge was built in the seventeenth century, and at that time there were at least six forges in that one shop. It was a big shop and reached halfway up Gold Street. When we took it over there were four forges and eventually I had them pulled down until the one original seventeenth century forge remained.

Wherever you see metalwork in Walden, that was done in our forge. We made all the railings on the houses in the High Street, and the street lamps – this is after I had started my own business; my father had retired by then. I made all the lamps in the Town Hall and all the steelwork in Walden church roof.

Hubert Bell

Cutting Barley

During the harvest the men hardly ever came home to a meal. We always had our meals brought to us and the farmer provided beer for us to drink. A lot of the corn – even then – was cut by hand. I can remember cutting barley by hand. We used a sickle. Instead of hitting at it, we would grab a few straws and pull and cut near to the ground. Beans were all cut by hand. There were more beans and peas grown for cattle food in those days.

There used to be eleven or twelve of us, and casual labour as well, working on the sugar beet. It was all lifted and loaded by hand. Now just two men do it, one on the machine and one driving the lorry. To thrash, cut and bale straw ten men were needed, now with the combine it is just a one man operation, isn't it?

Henry Moore (Ashdon)

Scrubbing

I worked at the Mansion. I went to work there the day after I left school

Mortimers Lane, Ashdon, 1890s.

at the age of fourteen. I was there eighteen months. I was the third housemaid. There was the butler and his wife and the housekeeper and two other housemaids and a nanny for the children. This would be in 1926. I used to get one Sunday off once a fortnight and half a day off a week. We slept on the top floor at the opposite end of the house to the family.

I worked hard. Some days I was scrubbing all day. They had oak stairs and they used to be scrubbed. I did mostly basic housework.

Kate Clark

The Refuse Cart

Working on the refuse cart was a very enjoyable job with the mates I got, we were a very good crew. I had some good companions. It was a very interesting job but a dirty job, but someone had to do it. You met some very good characters. The older people where you stopped and bid the time of day with them, they looked forward to seeing you every week. I think, really and truly it was one of the happiest jobs I did.

Kenny Clayden

Keeping Warm

Sometimes when you were working in the fields during the cold weather you would stand up against the horses to keep warm. Goldstones had sixteen or seventeen horses when I started work first. Or sometimes, you lit a fire in the

Springs Cottage, Water End, Ashdon, 1880s.

hedge and warmed your can and made some toast. You see, you would fill you can when you were at home, and if it was frosty it would be frozen by breakfast time. Breakfast was at nine.

Henry Moore (Ashdon)

The Nurseries

I worked at Engelmann's Nurseries until I got married. There wasn't anything else for me to do, it was either the nurseries or the laundry or going into service. I didn't like working in the nurseries. I don't like gardening and I don't like getting my hands dirty.

Ruby Piper

Baker's Boy

I was thirteen when I left school and I became a baker's boy for Mr Frost who had the bakery opposite the butcher's shop in Radwinter Road. (They are both private houses now.) Those were the days of horse-drawn carts. We also delivered coal and ran a hire service. We used to meet the trains at Ashdon Halt and Audley End with the wagonette or brougham. I started work in the morning at seven o'clock and never got home until about nine at night.

Gradually the horses disappeared and we had a motor to meet people at the station and a van to deliver the bread. But I missed the horses very much – they are lovely pets. But it was pell-mell

The Co-op in Victoria Avenue, 1940s.

all the time, extremely hard work with never a dull moment. We had to groom the horses and get them ready for work.

I lived in the bakery until I got married. My father complained that I didn't get home for my midday meal until half past two or three o'clock, because I had to meet the trains from the station. So Mr Frost said, 'Your boy had better have his meals at my house then', and my father said, 'Yes, I'll be glad to get his feet from under my table!'

I used to deliver bread to Great Mortimers. I would leave the pony and cart at the corner in Mortimers Lane and then walk across the fields to Great Mortimers. The lane was only a rough old cart track and the cart used to be swaying from side to side. There used to be four cottages at Water End, and I delivered bread three times a week and each house had about six or eight loaves

at a time and at weekend a peck of flour.

I was with Mr Frost for about three or four years and then Martins took over. They also had a bakery where the Labour Hall now stands and they took over and ran both bakeries. I was with the Martins until they closed in 1950 and then I went to work for Mr Lawrence Bidwell who took over and I stayed there until I retired early in 1972.

George Ford (Ashdon)

Long Hours

The Co-op in Victoria Avenue was a very small building next door to the bungalow. Len was manager, he used to work long hours. From eight-thirty in the morning until six at night, eight on Saturday nights. Later, in the 1960s, the

Young Pat Furze who later became Mrs George Witty.

shop was moved to the corner. He continued as manager for a while and then went on the grocery van, then he worked in the Castle Street Co-op.

Doris Reed

A Job at the Hospital

I took a six-month course of shorthand, typing and book-keeping with Mrs Fancett in Church Street and then I replied to an advertisement in the Saffron Walden Weekly for a shorthand typist to the Hospital Secretary, Miss Elizabeth Day. (This was in 1937.) After an interview with the House Committee Chairman, Mr Leonard Pitstow, I was appointed for the princely sum of £1 a week. The Matron at that time was Miss Parker who eventually married Mr Pitstow.

For the next eight years I cycled the eight and a half miles from Goldstones to the London Road every day. Sometimes I was accompanied by Len Cable who worked at the Pearl Assurance office at the corner of Church Street and High Street. I can't ever remember using the bus, but if there was a bus service, we lived too far out of Ashdon, it just wouldn't have been convenient. Sometimes I would get a lift home, someone would put my bike on top of their car or, on occasions, tow me home!

I had a half-day every Thursday but had to work all day Saturday. Miss Day and I worked in the Board Room, and I used a manual typewriter and eventually they installed a small telephone switchboard so that I could get straight through to the wards or Matron's office for patient enquiries. Sometimes I typed letters for the doctors as well as Miss Day, and I sent out notices for the various monthly committees. I also worked out the staff wages monthly and cycled down to Barclays in Market Place to collect the money, and then helped Miss Day to put up the money.

Once I had to cycle to Quenden Hall with a letter for Sir William Foot Mitchell who – I think – must have been Chairman of the Board of Governors at that time – but I'm not sure.

Miss Day was also in charge of the X-ray department which was opposite the board room and near the out-patients' department.

Pat Witty (Ashdon)

Matron and domestic staff at Saffron Walden General Hospital about 1938. Daisy Moore is at the extreme right.

Washing on the Common

My grandparents lived in Museum Court at the top of Museum Street. My grandmother used to hang her washing out on the Common. They used to go over there wearing sacking aprons and they would do the washing for the local gentry and hang it out on the Common.

Joy Waterman

Mangles

I left the Boys' British School at the age of fifteen in 1923 and went to Jennings as the office boy. This was in Mr Ernest Jennings' time, and I ended up as one of the partners.

I used to go to the market auctions every Tuesday. The first Tuesday in each month we had a sale in which we sold everything and anything from a bike to a motor car or mangles, kitchen fenders. This was on the Pig Market site. At Christmas time we used to have a thousand turkeys to auction and if they made 10d or 1s a pound we thought they were doing well. This was in the late 1920s or early '30s.

John Barker

Ambition

I left the Boys' British School in 1933 at the age of fourteen and went as a trainee to a gents' hairdresser in the Central Arcade. My wages were 5s a

Watson's Christmas turkey sale, 1940s.

week the first year and 7s 6d the second and 10s the third year. I left to better myself and went to work for Mr Tom Pope in the Market Place and I got £1 a week.

I had six years with Mr Pope and then I started up on my own in 1939. My father started me. He bought and furnished and equipped me. The premises were in the High Street next door to Sketchley's.

I remember the first Saturday on my own in business. I was working from eight in the morning until eight at night and I went home with £1 4s. I had had a very busy day and I went home as proud as a peacock. That was in the

days when a haircut was 6d. When I retired haircuts were £1.60.

In the early days I used to shave people. I used to go to the Friends' School to cut the children's hair and to Debden to cut the RAF officers' hair, and the Isolation Hospital in Landscape View. They were mostly TB patients up there, and one or two infectious diseases.

We moved in 1951 to where the Gun Shop is – No. 17 – it was Mr Edgar the dentist's place. I kept on until 1983 and then I decided to retire after 51 years of work.

Arthur Norman

CLIFTON
BOARDING HOUSE

HIGH STREET
Saffron Walden

BED & BREAKFAST

Personal Supervision.
Proprietress: Mrs. VERT

Running Hot and Cold Water in
Bedrooms. 'Phone 186

Advertisement for The Clifton Boarding House, now Saffron Walden Motors.

Undertaking

My father started in business in 1910 building houses for Bill Goddard of the Neville Arms. He started with a horse and cart, using a hand-cart for local jobs, later in 1917 he had a Model T Ford van with foot gears. We started undertaking about 1922; all the local builders in the villages did a spot of undertaking.

Ron Cain (Wendens Ambo)

Lady of the Manor

When I left school at fourteen I went into service, first at Wicken House, then I went to London and war was declared so I came back and I was in service at Mrs Stebbing Leverett's house in the High Street in Saffron Walden. Then I went to work at the boarding house across the road – Clifton House – I think it is a motor-car showroom now.

Mrs Bramwell Jackson lived at Wicken House when I went there. She was quite the lady of the manor. She had a lady's maid, a nursemaid, a parlourmaid and I was the kitchen maid and there were two or three gardeners. I lived in and we had to get up early. At six o'clock in the morning I was scrubbing the front steps.

Betty Dennison (Wicken Bonhunt)

The Big Slump

I started school at the Boys' British and I finished up at the Grammar School. After I left school I went to Colchester and was apprenticed to a marine

Advert for the Crawley Agrimotor Company, 1933. Note the telephone number, 17!

engineering firm. I wanted to go into the Merchant Navy. After I finished my apprenticeship it was the big slump of 1922 and so I came home and spent a bit of time helping my father with his secretarial work. Then I got a job at Crawley Agrimotors, it was just after my father died in 1923 and I could not leave home because my sister was married, my brother working away and my mother was almost blind.

I was at Crawley Agrimotors ten years and then things were bad again and I was 'put off' and I landed up with Cleales. I was there for thirty years until I retired in 1970 at the age of seventy. I was in Gold Street until they moved and then they moved up to Station Road.

Charlie Shepherd

Rags

My father was a road man, and he had his length of road from the bottom of Gunters Hill to the Fox and Hounds – this side of Thaxted – it was about seven miles. In frosty weather he used to tie rags to his feet so that he wouldn't slip. He used to trim the edges of the road, and he worked from seven o'clock in the morning until about five-thirty. On Saturday mornings he used to sweep the village up.

William Swan (Wimbish)

Three Generations

When I left the Boys' British I went to De Barrs and remained there the whole time. I worked for three generations of the De Barr family. I did the boot and shoe repairs on the premises. When I first started repairing shoes the majority of the footwear was very clumsy looking and now everything is stuck on and sewn and stitched. The shoes were much heavier in the old days.

Henry Bacon

Humane Killer

Generally my father carried a humane killer (a special gun) in his car along with other veterinary paraphernalia. I have seen many animals beyond remedial treatment killed with this instrument. On one occasion, at a farm, a shire horse suffered a broken leg, meaning the poor thing had to be put down. Unfortunately the humane killer was not in the car, so father had to resort to borrowing a double-barrelled gun from the farmer. Father lined himself up a few paces from the horse which was standing amazingly placidly, fired and killed it instantly.

Cattle were difficult to kill on account of their solidly constructed foreheads. I recall an occasion when the bullet from the gun ricocheted off a bull's head merely stunning the animal. A second bullet was needed.

Castration was often a conveyor belt type of operation especially with the likes of pigs and lambs. A register of swine castration had to be kept and presented to the police. The only animal that was given an anaesthetic for castration was a dog, which entailed delicate handling during and afterwards.

Domestic animals – cats, dogs, pets etc. – did not figure greatly in our

Local vet Percy Welch with his son in the driving seat, talking to his brother, farmer Harry Welch, at Springwell Farm.

practice, although my father was rapidly paying more attention to this profitable field at the time I left home permanently in the 1940s. Today, of course, a vet could not survive without catering for pets and small animals.

Farmers in general were very slow to pay their bills. It took many reminders, even sometimes County Court threats to bring the cheque books out. Lots of people, particularly the poorer farm labourers, would often pay in kind with vegetables etc. My grandfather was generous in the extreme, letting some struggling people have free treatment for their animals. He would dispense many of his own medicines, lotions and

Strawberry picking at Water End, Ashdon, late 1890s. Margaret Cornell is fourth from the left and Mr Charlton is holding the dog.

liniments. A popular prescription of his was embrocation (sometimes called white oils by locals) a highly pungent but effective muscle stimulant. Local football teams and clubs would get bottles of the stuff from him and, as he knew I played for the Saffron Walden Football Club and also took part in sports in general, he was most reluctant to take any money for the product.

Captain C.J. Welch

The Strawberry Field

My mother's father worked on the land for Mr Frederick Furze and my grandmother used to work in the strawberry field down at Water End. It was Mr Charlton's strawberry field and it ran right down Stallantine along by White Cottage right along to the

Wilderness. They also used to make jam in a little hut up there. One of my aunts – Ada Cornell (later she became Ada Cardy) was Mr Charlton's chauffeuse, she got her first driving licence in 1923.

Dorothy Bartlett (Ashdon)

Horse-keepers

All the horse-keepers used to comb their horses' tails and they could keep the loose hair which they would sell. If a horse wouldn't stand still whilst you were plaiting its tail, you would back it up to the stable door and get the other side of the door so that it wouldn't kick you. A tablespoonful of arsenic gives a lovely shine to a horse's coat. So does stale beer.

William Swan (Wimbish)

The little hut at Springfield, Ashdon, where they made the strawberry jam, 1890s.

In Service

I was born in Ashdon in 1913, and when I was thirteen years old I went straight to the Bells at No. 11 Mount Pleasant Road in Saffron Walden. It was Mr William Bell, the father of L'Argent. At that time L'Argent was a grown man working at the office with his father. William's wife's name was Sarah. They had two children, Phyllis and L'Argent. Phyllis by this time was already married. She married a Mr Knockolds. So there were just three members of the Bell family living at No. 11 – William, Sarah and L'Argent.

There were five bedrooms, attics and cellars – we slept in the attic. I was house parlourmaid, and there was a cook – she also slept in. We shared the work between us. It was very hard work but I was very happy there. I started work at seven in the morning, and my

first duties were cleaning the kitchen fireplace out. We had a coal range and a gas cooker to cook on. All the rooms had beautiful cast-iron open fires, and brass fire-irons and fire dogs which all had to be cleaned of course.

First of all I had to clean out the grates. The cook made the breakfast whilst I set the table and took the breakfast in. They used to have breakfast about half-past eight because L'Argent and his father used to be at the office by nine o'clock.

The cook and I used to work together. Whilst she was preparing the dinners I used to be upstairs making the beds and cleaning the rooms. First of all we had a carpet sweeper and then we had something called a 'housemaid'. Yes, there was a lot of polishing and dusting. We would do a couple of bedrooms perhaps one day and a couple the next. They had wash basins in all the

65

Wimbish Green at the turn of the century.

bedrooms with brass taps which had to be polished. There was only one bathroom. We used to use the back staircase. We used to get into their bedrooms to clean from the back staircase.

We would finish after washing up the lunch things and then we used to rest until half past four, then they would have a light tea about five o'clock – tea, bread and butter, jam and cake – and then they would have dinner about seven clock in the evening. We would finish our work about eight to eight-thirty.

I had half a day off in the week and half a day every other Sunday. I either used to walk or cycle home to Holden End in Ashdon. Often we would walk there in the afternoon and come back on the train. It was a lovely little train. My dad would walk back to the station with me.

William Bell's wife died and Edith Bell, his sister, came back to keep house for William and L'Argent. After L'Argent got married, the cook left and Edith had a home of her own, and there was only me left then, but L'Argent's wife used to help me with the housework.

The whole family were very nice to me. After L'Argent got married there was only L'Argent and Olive (his wife) and I was treated as one of the family, especially after their daughter, Elizabeth, was born. They used to take me out picnicking with then. We took the big car out into the country and sometimes we would go blackberrying.

I'm glad I have been in service. It taught me how to behave. You learn how to do things. It made me feel different somehow. When I left in 1942 they were still living at No. 11 Mount Pleasant Road. I would not have left but I had no choice, as I had to do war service.

Doris Bibby

Cottages in Thaxted Road, Wimbish, 1930s.

Church on Good Friday

I worked from six in the morning until five-thirty six days a week. The only holiday we got paid for was Christmas Day. If you didn't go to work on Boxing Day you were 'set off' (not paid). If you didn't go to church on Good Friday you didn't get paid. They used to say the man was more in fear of his master than God. If you went to church you had the rest of the day off!

William Swan (Wimbish)

Parlourmaid

When I left school I trained as a parlourmaid. I went to a large house called Plaw Hatch, it's a boarding school now. Plaw Hatch was owned by Mr and Mrs Prior. They had seven servants and seven gardeners. I was there for several years and when I left I went to Mr and Mrs Walter Gold at Stansted. I was there until I married in 1940. I lived in and I enjoyed it. It was a good home and they were very, very nice people. I did love Walter Gold, he was a dear old man, but so economical! I had to be downstairs by six-thirty in the morning to catch the morning mail. If I wasn't there the postman would take it back. We didn't finish work until after the evening meal, so we usually got to bed about nine o'clock.

Irene Hudgell (Arkesden)

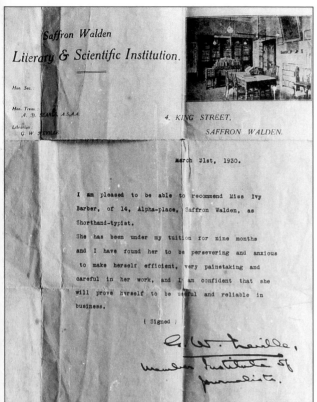

Saffron Walden
Literary & Scientific Institution.

Hon. Sec.:

Hon. Treas.:
A. B. SEARLE, A.S.A.A.

Librarian:
G. W. DEVILLE

4, KING STREET,
SAFFRON WALDEN.

March 31st, 1930.

I am pleased to be able to recommend Miss Ivy
Barber, of 14, Alpha-place, Saffron Walden, as
Shorthand-typist.
She has been under my tuition for nine months
and I have found her to be persevering and anxious
to make herself efficient, very painstaking and
careful in her work, and I am confident that she
will prove herself to be useful and reliable in
business.

(Signed)

Ivy Brown's (née Barber) reference from the
Librarian at Saffron Walden Literary and
Scientific Institution.

A Lackey for Everyone

After I left school I went to work at Westleys Farm for 10s a week. It was owned by Mr Bruty then. I worked seven days a week. On Sundays I had to milk the house cow twice a day and feed the pigs. I started on the stock and then on to horses. I used to lead the horses out to the field and when I got bigger we were trusted to drive them away. You were a lackey for everyone, you had to accept it, there was nothing else to do. There used to be three men on the farm and I was the boy.

William Swan (Wimbish)

The Job I Wanted

I went to South Road School until I was twelve years old and then I went to the National School in Castle Street. I was fourteen when I left and my mother found me a position in service in a house in Landscape View, but I refused to go into service, so I went to Engelmann's to pack flowers. While I was working there I decided that I wanted to work in an office, but because I couldn't write shorthand or type, no one would have me. So I decided to learn, and I went to the librarian at the library who taught shorthand and typing. He taught me and I was qualified in nine months, and so I got the job I wanted. Shorthand and typing came easily to me.

I went to Crawley Agrimotors. This would be about 1930. It was a very small office, there was one other girl besides me. It was a small factory and all they had for the office accommodation was one office for the boss and one for the typist. I got 11s a week and we worked from eight-thirty until one o'clock and then two until six. Saturdays was from nine until twelve-thirty. We always went home for lunch.

Then Crawley Agrimotors went broke and from there I went to Spicers at Sawston, but at that time they didn't have a vacancy and I had to work in the factory – which I hated! (But you were lucky to get a job in those days.) After two days I went to the boss and asked if I could work in the office and he told me there was no vacancy but he would bear it in mind, and it was only three months later that they had a vacancy and they gave it me on three months' trial. After three months I was made permanent and I stayed there for eleven years. After that I went to an estate agent in Cambridge but I did not stay there long before I went to the Ministry of Agriculture and Fisheries.

Ivy Brown

Taken From School

Mr Arthur Crawley Snr, who owned Yews Farm in Hadstock, was also a school manager and went into the school one day and spoke to the mistress and then said to my mother-in-law, 'Come along my dear, you have finished school now.' He said, 'Your sister has had to go home to look after your mother and you are to come and work for me in her place.' She was literally taken from school and she had to go and get her clothes.

They had four young children at Yews Farm and she was up at six o'clock in the morning to get the water for Mr Crawley to shave so that he could go out and meet the men at seven o'clock. Then she had to help Mrs Crawley with the work and she was lucky if she had got done at nine o'clock at night. She had Sunday afternoon and Sunday evening off and was paid 5s a week.

Reg Wood (Hadstock)

An Old-fashioned Farmer

I was born in Wendens Ambo, my father worked for Mr Harry Duke. Mr Duke was an old-fashioned farmer. I was

Farmer Harry Duke watching his men at work in Wendens Ambo, early 1930s.

working on the farm before I left school, leading the horses into the field and putting up the stooks, and then, because I was big for my age, they let me drive away from the field with the empty wagons.

It was a good life. During wet weather we used to have a sack under the bushes to keep it dry whilst the other one was being worn over our shoulders. (This was in the 1930s.)

During harvest time we used to work until it got dark. It lasted for about six weeks of the year, and they gave us a five pound bonus, but I was only a boy so I got half of that.

In my time on the farm you took a pride in your work. You had to put the

69

Mr Wilfred Dennis, a Saffron Walden postman, who lost his arm during the 1914 war.

Antiques

When I left Wimbish School I went to Saffron Walden into service. I first worked at Ingleside House for Mr Trew and then I went to work for Mrs William Bell at Saffron Lodge in Mount Pleasant Road. It was a house full of antiques. I lived in at both places. I could not visit home until I had saved enough money to buy a bike. We used to go home once a fortnight. The Trews had two live-in maids, but at the Bells, Flo Evans came in daily. We used to have to be up soon after six.

Ida Swan (Wimbish)

The Telephone Exchange

I went to the village school and when I left I helped my father on his smallholding for a while, and then I went to work at the telephone exchange in Radwinter until I married. This was about 1936 and there were between twenty-five and thirty people on the phone in those days. They were mostly farmers. It was a manual exchange and you had to tell people when their three minutes were up. Everything was done by hand – you had to wait until people were connected, so you could not help but overhear a bit of their conversation. But most of the time we were far too busy to listen in.

We had the post office as well. Mrs Potts and her daughter Nellie ran the post office. The village was alive then. The post office was open from seven o'clock in the morning until six at night. The men would call in for their Woodbines on their way to work.

sheaves just so on the wagons. Sometimes there would be half a dozen men hoeing by hand. It was surprising how much ground you covered. When they lifted the sugar beet, you had to knock the soil off. There used to be ten or twelve men and six teams of horses. We used to plough with wooden ploughs. It was quite hard work. We used to cut the hedges and trim the grass round with a 'bagging hook' (hand sickle).

Clifford Richardson

The post office sold sweets but it was not a money-order post office. Nellie's brother Freddie was the postman and he also used to mend shoes in a little shed at the bottom of the garden. At Christmas the post would come over by horse and cart from Saffron Walden, there were so many parcels. And of course in those days the postmen wore hard hats.

We used to walk with the telegrams. We used to get 1½d to walk to Wimbish Hall – it is about a mile each way. If I wasn't too busy I would go, but there were other people also willing to deliver the telegrams, and of course, in those days there were quite a lot of telegrams because so few people were on the phone.

Joyce Jarvis (Radwinter)

Sixpence for the Horse

When I worked for Mr Bruty I used to go to Saffron Walden Market with a few chickens and a pig. I used to go up to the Railway Arms and stable the horse. It was 6d for the horse, and I had 1s for my lunch. This would be about 1920. The auctioneer used to give me 3d, but he didn't give me the money, he wrote it on a slip of paper and I'd take it to the White Horse and they'd give me half a pint of beer. If I wanted more I had to pay for it myself.

William Swan (Wimbish)

George Swann on a Fowler steam engine.

The Cook Boy

I started with the steam plough engines at the age of fifteen. This was 1928. On the steam plough engines you have to start as a 'van boy' or 'cook boy' – in Suffolk you were known as a 'van boy'. There used to be five of us in a team for steam ploughing. The cook boy had to cook for four men, which wasn't a very thankful job. One man probably wanted his bacon cooked nice and crisp, while another just wanted it put in the pan and turned over. It was a job to satisfy them. You had to be up before everyone else. We used to work from light until dark. The cook boy had to be up to get a cup of tea ready in the morning. We just lived in that van for five days at a

71

Steam ploughing at Wimbish, 1940s.

time. The vans were big ones on steel wheels and they carried all the tools and everything to maintain steam ploughs.

In the van you had a fireplace right opposite the door. There was a table running down the centre of the van with flaps either side. At night the table flaps would be put down, and the flaps on the bunks put up. A man used to sleep either side, one man at one end and the foreman used to sleep at the other end and the cook boy wherever he could. You took your own sheet if you wanted one. It was a rough life but a happy life. We all worked as one team. We never had a row, and I enjoyed it.

I was cook boy for a year and then I was a steerer – I used to steer the implements. There used to be one steam engine one side of the field and another the other side, with a cable between them and they would pull backwards and forwards from one end of the field to another, and that worked the plough. We used to have about 800 yards of steel rope.

Even when you were a cook boy you had to drive the engine, because they never stopped from when they started in the morning until it went dark in the evening, not even for meals. So you had to get on the engine and release the drive while the other man ate his meals.

When we were steam ploughing in summer we used to work until three-thirty on Saturdays. For all the extra acres you did you got a 1d an acre. The drivers used to get 35s a week plus 5d an acre. The foreman – I never knew what his standard wage was but he would get 6d an acre. When I was steering I got 32s a week and 4d an acre. I have no regrets at all.

George Swann

Finchingfield in the 1930s.

The New Time

We used to walk to Finchingfield school and walk back and then we had to help with the animals after school. I left school at the end of the First War. One of my jobs was to take the horses to Mr Gouldstone the blacksmith in Great Sampford to be shod. By this time British Summer Time had come in. Everyone called it 'the new time' and went by that. But the blacksmith and the farm labourers used to go by the 'old time'. So we had plenty of time after school to help on the farm.

Fred Brook (Little Sampford)

A Lyons Nippy

After leaving school at the age of thirteen I went to work at Engelmann's for a time and then I went to live in London. It was my ambition to become a Lyons 'Nippy' because I liked the uniform – a brown dress with a frilly apron and cap. I didn't become a Nippy because I wasn't tall enough, I was only about 5 ft 1½ ins and they wanted taller girls. But by this time the war had started – the First War – so I sat the Civil Service exam and went into the War Office, and stayed in London until the war ended.

Molly Porter

Ron Rust.

Loading Trees

I remember we were loading trees one Saturday morning – we used to pile them up really high – and the chain unhooked itself and rolled down and knocked down the fence of a nearby house. Old William Bell was sitting in his office watching us and saw us smash the fence. The old chap used to give us 2s every week if we had done a good week's work. And this week I remember him saying, 'Well, no five-eighths washers for you this week!' (A florin – two shillings – was about the size of a five-eighths washer.)

Loading trees was very hard and dangerous work. But so long as you knew how to do it, and if you worked as a team and the bloke on the engine knew every signal you gave and knew

exactly what you wanted, you were all right.

George Swann

The Old Bakehouse

I went to Radwinter School and left when I was fourteen to go to work for Mr Bill Spittle the baker who had his bakery in part of the Brewery Tavern. In those days they served tea and cakes at the back. This was wartime. I always liked cooking. I used to work at the bakery on Saturdays and at nights long before I left school. My job was to wash and grease all the tins ready for next day.

The cottage next door to the Brewery Tavern is still called The Old Bakehouse. I have done some gardening for the people who live there and their bedrooms are over the top of the cellars where we used to keep the fat and jams. In those days we did nearly everything by hand. All the bread was moulded by hand. I used to do 5,000 jam tarts a day. They had about eight or nine vans on the road.

Mr Spittle was a Londoner and took over the bakery at the beginning of the war. It had been a bakery for a long time but they only made bread in those early days. The bread was baked in an old-fashioned 'faggot' oven. That means faggots were put into the oven first to heat it. There was a gauge on the outside and when the oven was the right temperature, the burning ash had to be swept out and the bread put in.

I worked at the bakery for five and a half years, until I had to do my National Service. I went into the army as a baker and ended up as a cook. When I came out of the army in 1952 I went to work at the Rose and Crown in Saffron Walden, but the hours were rather awkward for someone who didn't live in Saffron Walden. So then I went to work for Mr Andrews in the High Street (later it became Coles) and we used to help out Mr Anthony, another local baker. Then I went to work for Millers in London Road. I left Millers to work for the Highways Department and I was there for the next twenty-three years until I retired for health reasons.

Ron Rust (Radwinter)

Bunching Flowers

I went to South Road school and when I left I went to Engelmann's to work for a short while. I used to bunch flowers for 2s 6d a week. We started at eight o'clock in the morning until five o'clock in the evening and I walked all the way from Pleasant Valley and back.

Then I went into service because there weren't many other jobs for girls. I went to work for the Miss Winters in South Road and I stayed with them until they died. They died within a week of each other. I was there when Queen Wilhelmina and Princess Juliana of Holland visited. I had the privilege of getting tea for them. That was September 9th 1935. Yes, it was quite a thrill! Miss Saxton Winter had been chaperone to Queen Wilhelmina when she was a young girl, and Miss Nance had been Matron at Walden Place during the First War.

Ellen Banks

Queen Wilhelmina and Princess Juliana of Holland visiting the Miss Winters in 1935.

Long Hours

I started hairdressing straight from school. I was apprenticed for three years to Mr Albert Watts in King Street where Mr Williams the optician is now. That was in 1935. After my three years was up I went to work for Mr Dennis in Hill Street where my son is now. Jimmie Dennis opened his shop in 1919. I had just over two years with him and then war broke out. What happened was, Jimmie and I got on exceptionally well together and he said that if ever he sold the business he would give me first chance. Which he did, in 1945, and I got back from the war in 1946, and he held the business until I got back and

Mr Wells' cycle shop in the High Street, 1920s.

then he stayed with me for six months.

The hours were longer in those days and styles have changed a lot. In the old days you used to get men in for a daily shave. There is no shaving now. It is all hair. In the old days we would shave with a cut-throat razor. When I was with Mr Watts, Mr Land used to come in from Adams & Land, the solicitors. Mr Land used to come in to Mr Albert Watts and Mr Adams was a customer of Jimmie's, and he used to shave in the hairdresser's every day.

Tuesdays were very busy days in those days. We got lots of the local farmers in. We knew all the local farmers because we were so near to the market.

Cyril Swan

CHAPTER 5
Leisure

Off to Newmarket races. Mr McKay is driving, with Mr Lawrence the landlord in shirt sleeves, at the rear of the Railway Inn.

Dorothy Bartlett in the meadows she roamed as a child.

Food for Free

On Sunday afternoons we would go out to pick wild strawberries. What a lot we had to pick to get enough for one small dish for tea! But, oh, they were delicious. There was also lovely fresh watercress growing in a stream at Water End.

Dorothy Bartlett (Ashdon)

Sunday

Sundays had to be an easy day. Father was out in the garden and probably was there until we had dinner. We had to do the washing up afterwards and then we always went out as a family. We might walk round to Littlebury, Audley End Park or Audley End Village. Sometime we used to go to one or other of father's sisters, who had married farmers, for a cup of tea.

Margaret McGowan

Sunday School

We were always made to go to the Baptist Chapel Sunday School on Sunday mornings – my parents were very strict. My father could read the Bible almost all the way through.

Fred Goodwin (Ashdon)

Sunday Evenings

Mum was the youngest of Thomas and Alice Kidman's nine children. She recalls Sunday evenings around the fire, reading the Bible and the family singing hymns. Her father's favourites were 'The Old Rugged Cross' and 'Oh Happy Day that fixed my choice in Thee my Saviour and my God'.

John Maddams

Bible

My grandfather, George Cornell, was a Baptist. He used to be a Lay Reader and on Sunday afternoons he used to have a little gathering on the bridge at Water End. He would take his big Bible with him to read from.

Dorothy Bartlett (Ashdon)

Sissy

When we were children we used to play around the farms and in the meadows. The farmers didn't mind us playing around the farm just as long as we behaved ourselves. In summer we spent half our time paddling in the river. Children couldn't do that now – it's too polluted! We used to go bird's-nesting – but if our headmaster found out we were in real trouble. We used to pick violets. It sounds sissy now, but all the children did it in those days. We also used to make trucks out of old pram wheels.

Eddie Clayden (Little Chesterford)

Sunday School

Sundays were spent at Sunday School, at ten fifteen in the morning, then

George Cornell, the Baptist lay reader at Ashdon, late 1890s.

church at eleven, chapel at three o'clock and church again at six-thirty. My parents made me go, I didn't like it very much but everyone else was the same.

Ron Cain (Wendens Ambo)

Nothing Special

We used to make our own fun. Sport came as the seasons came along. We made our own football and cricket – we had cricket things but they were nothing special.

When we were at school we used to play Ashdon School at football. There

Albert Rowlandson, Hadstock.

up to Newport Road were on fire. One Sunday mother tied my hair back in one thick plait, it was so hot. It was a thing that was unheard of in those days; on Sunday, you always wore your hair loose.

Ellen Banks

Nylons

I was captain of the ladies' football team for the laundry for the Festival of Britain. We beat Engelmann's ladies' team and Castle Street Laundry. Jack Southall, the laundry owner, was very generous, he gave us all one pound each and a pair of nylon stockings. He bought new football boots for us to play in and gave them to the boys' school at Shudy Camps afterwards.

Alice Clayden

was nothing in the village but you didn't take any notice because you didn't know any difference. We always used to go to Saffron Walden to the cinema. There used to be two cinemas there. There was more entertainment in wartime.

I used to sing in the church choir morning and night and go to Sunday School in the afternoon. Going to church was part of the social life.

Albert Rowlandson (Hadstock)

Dances

There used to be quite a lot going on in the village. During the war we had films in the Village Hall for the troops which were stationed here. We used to have dances in the school, which is now closed, and whist drives for the older people. And we used to go to the pictures in Saffron Walden three or four times a week.

Cyril Perrin (Littlebury)

The Summer of '21

I remember that hot July in 1921. All the corn fields from Pleasant Valley

The W.I.

We started our W.I. on 1 December 1949. When we started, the

Cyril Perrin, Littlebury.

whole village joined – we had as many as forty-five members – but now, of course, it is totally different. I am the only founder-member left.

Irene Hudgell (Arkesden)

A Season for all Games

We had our hoops or sometimes an old bicycle wheel. We always used to play marbles and conkers. There was a season for all games.

Jim Surrey

Fish and Chips

We used to bike into Walden. In those days there were two cinemas. We would go into the cheapest seats – 9d – and finish off at Frank Bacon's for fish and chips.

Edgar Moss (Ashdon)

Harvest Time

It was exciting when the corn was cut. We would take our sticks and walk round the edge of the field for rabbits when they ran out. Then after all the sheaves had gone out of the fields we knew it was alright to glean corn for our chickens. If there was a sheaf in the middle of the field we knew that one wasn't to be gleaned. Our mother would pack up some sandwiches and drinks and we would spend the day gleaning.

Once after the harvest we were riding on top of a trailer-load of straw pulled along by a tractor when suddenly it went over a bump and the top half of

What is your WORRY?

FORGET IT!——————

AND SEE THE PROGRAMME AT THE

WALDEN CINEMA

HIGH STREET
SAFFRON WALDEN
Telephone 205

TIMES OF PERFORMANCES:
MONDAY to FRIDAY—
CONTINUOUS FROM 6 p.m.

SATURDAYS, AND BANK HOLIDAYS—
3 Separate Houses at 2.15, 5.50 & 8.25 p.m.

FREE CAR PARK

Walden Cinema advert, 1938.

the load slid off with us with it. We all went down under some barbed wire and down into a ditch, but nobody was hurt.

Dorothy Bartlett (Ashdon)

Cherry Brandy

I belonged to The Band of Hope when it was at the Quaker Meeting House at the top of the High Street. I had signed the pledge and more or less kept to it, except that I loved the occasional drop of cherry brandy.

Molly Porter

Driving Cattle

We used to go to the market when school was over and we would drive the cattle from the market up to the station and put them on the wagons and load them on the train. There was quite a number of them. Mr Coe was a farmer up in Peaslands Road where the Leisure Centre is now. He was a dealer in cattle and he would buy a lot of bullocks and then we used to drive them up to the farm. We didn't get paid – we did it because it was fun.

Jim Surrey

Gleaning

I remember when we went gleaning when we were children. My mother used to cook the day before and we would spend all our summer holidays doing it. She used to take a thing called a 'truck' (a little cart on wheels) and we used to take sacks. She also made us little sacks which we tied around us and the heads of corn were put straight into one sack and the ones with straw we held in our hands and when we had enough we would tie a straw around them and put them in the other sack.

I used to love gleaning. We used to have such lovely weather in those days. You were never allowed to go into a field until they had put a shock in the middle – six sheaves of corn placed together. You had to wait for that to be put in the middle of the field before you could go in and glean.

Mollie Moore (Ashdon)

Little Mollie Moore (née Player) with her big sister, Bessie.

White Ribboners

Mrs Custerson used to run lots of little things in the town and she ran one thing called the White Ribboners. It was an organization for children between the ages of eight and sixteen, and one of the things it promoted was alcoholic abstinence because Mrs Custerson was a die-hard against drink.

When I was a White Ribboner she asked me if I would like to come and help her make mince pies. She said she was going to make every resident in the Union (Workhouse) a mince pie for Christmas. She said, 'That will be 150. I will get my cook to make the pastry, and I will cut them out and you can put the mincemeat into them'.

Frieda Hobbs

The Girls' Friendly Society

I was in the Girls' Friendly Society. We had meetings at Brick House. We used to do sewing and Miss Pollitt would read to us. She used to play the organ at church and I used to sing in the choir.

Betty Dennison (Wicken Bonhunt)

Mr William Thake at the Essex Show, 1957.

The Agricultural Show

Outings were limited but, if possible, father would take mother and me to the annual Agricultural Show. It was a lovely day out. We used to take sandwiches and mother would make something special in the cake line. And it was so nice to dress up in clothes that were kept for special occasions. Father loved it because he would see lots of his mates that he'd worked with on the different farms.

Margaret Rust (Radwinter)

Old Swimming Bath

The old swimming bath in Hill Street was a great favourite with us young boys – David Miller, Peter Balaam, Eric Porter and many others – all members of the swimming club. I suppose I was most successful at football, being a regular member of the Saffron Walden Town football team at the age of barely fourteen. Each week it was quite a thrill to look for my name in the Saffron Walden Weekly News football reports of the previous week's match. That was 1940 or so.

Captain C.J. Welch

Borough of Saffron Walden
PUBLIC BATHS,
HILL STREET.

Time Table and Tariff of Charges.
Subject to Alteration.

SWIMMING BATH.

			TIME.	PRICES.
Monday ...	Gentlemen	...	7 to 9 a.m.	6d.
	Ladies	...	10 a.m. to 1 p.m.	,,
	Gentlemen	...	2 to 9 p.m.	,,
Tuesday ...	Gentlemen	...	7 to 1 p.m.	,,
	Ladies ...	...	2 to 4 p.m.	,,
	Gentlemen	...	5 to 9 p.m.	,,
Wednesday	Gentlemen	...	7 to 1 p.m.	,,
	,,	...	2 to 4 p.m.	,,
	Ladies ..	...	5 to 9 p.m.	,,
Thursday ...	Gentlemen	...	7 to 9 a.m.	4d.
	Ladies	...	10 a.m. to 1 p.m.	,,
	Gentlemen	...	2 to 9 p.m.	,,
Friday ...	Gentlemen	...	7 a.m. to 1 p.m.	,,
	,,	...	2 to 4 p.m.	,,
	Ladies	...	5 to 9 p.m.	,,
Saturday ...	Gentlemen	...	7 a.m. to 1 p.m.	,,
	,,	...	2 to 10 p.m.	2d.

6d. Tickets includes 2 Towels ; 4d. and 2d. Tickets include 1 Towel.
Bathing Drawers and Ladies Costumes 1d. extra. Extra Towel 1d.
Children under 13 half-price.
Book of 6d. Tickets 5s. per dozen. Book of 4d. Tickets 3s. 6d. per dozen.
SEASON TICKETS :—Ladies or Gentlemen, 21s., available for 12 months, when the Bath is open to the Public.
Winter months the Bath will open at 8 a.m., and close at 8 p.m., except Saturdays at 9 p.m.

PRIVATE BATHS.

The Baths are open during the hours above named at the following charges :—
BATH—Hot or Cold (with Shower, including 2 Towels) 6d., (or 5s. per dozen tickets.)
BATH—Hot or Cold (including 1 Towel) 4d., (or 3s. 6d. per dozen tickets.)
Saturdays after 2 p.m., (including 1 Towel) 2d.

No person allowed to remain in the Baths more than 1 hour, without extra charge.
No Admission within 20 minutes of closing time.
THE COUNCIL reserve the right to appropriate certain days during the Season for Swimming Entertainments, &c., to which the Public will be admitted at special charges (and of which due notice will be given.)
Any Communications or enquiries with reference to the Baths, to be sent to
A. H. FORBES, Borough Surveyor.

Tariff for Saffron Walden Public Swimming Bath, 1910.

Mr Frederick Furze taking his family for a drive in the Austin, 1920s.

Swimming

We used to make our own amusement. I remember when I was a boy we used to block up the river until we had five or six feet of water and then we would strip off and pretend to be swimming.

Fred Goodwin (Ashdon)

Footballers and Cricketers

We were nearly all footballers and cricketers in Audley End Village. Most of the boys played for the town later. There was an Audley End cricket team and our father used to be in that. In those days there was a match going on each side of the road. The Village played one side of the A11 and Littlebury played in front of the Mansion.

Cyril Swan

Picnics by the River

We used to go for picnics by the river. A favourite spot was the Wilderness at Water End. Sometimes we would go in for a paddle. The weather always seemed to be hot and sunny in those days.

We would go fishing for tiddlers with a jam jar with a piece of string around the top to form a carrying handle and a length of stick with a net made from a piece of stocking or net curtain.

Dorothy Bartlett (Ashdon)

85

Toys

One of my earliest memories is of the kitchen where my father rigged up a fold-away table. It was a flap of wood attached to the wall which folded down when not in use. And my brother Roy and I would put out toy cars, farmyard animals and soldiers on it. We would play there for ages.

John Maddams

The Old Bath Chair

I couldn't afford a bike, but my pal and I used to go down to the tip and make up old bikes from bits and pieces. One day I saw an old bath chair up at the tip and we decided we would have a fight and the winner would get possession of the bath chair. I won the fight and I got the bath chair, but we used to share it.

I used to take the bath chair to school. All the boys had new bicycles but my parents couldn't afford that, but all the boys wanted to ride in the old bath chair so I rode on their new bikes!

Jim Surrey

Camps

We made camps in the hedgerows, and took our dolls and dolls' prams out to play with. The boys used to make go-carts from old pram wheels and pieces of wood, with a long thick piece of string tied to either side of the front axle to steer.

Dorothy Bartlett (Ashdon)

The Scouts

Just before and at the start of the Second War the Scouts was a good organization to belong to, providing us with weekend camps in the country, under the guidance of an Australian scoutmaster, Wally Everatt. All it entailed was marvellous, including the huge scout camp and gatherings at Shortgrove.

Activities during weekdays included two groups of youths setting out in the pitch darkness in opposite directions only to meet somewhere on the A11 road. The object being to collect as many neck scarves as possible from your rivals before returning to base at the High Street YMCA. Some of the midway meetings were a little on the brutal side. Not surprising really, because some of us would tie our scarves to our belts in order not to lose them.

Captain C.J. Welch

Embroidery

We used to have village hops and I played for them. My sister, Ruth, and I didn't go out much in those days. We were not allowed a radio until I was eighteen because of the music practice which had to go on every day. We used to do a lot of embroidery and occasionally we went to the pictures in Saffron Walden. But we were quite content. We used to go out for walks – that was the thing to do.

Joyce Jarvis (Radwinter)

Ron Cain with his B.S.C. Three Wheeler, 1950s.

A Busy Time

In the summer, harvest time was a busy time. We had to take tea to the men up in the fields and then we would have a ride on the horse and cart. We were happy and we made our own fun in those days. Most of the village life was centred around the pub and the church and we used to know everyone in the village. We used to have a curfew every night at eight o'clock. You had to go indoors when the bell was rung. They used to say that when the bell tolls the children used to go to bed and the men went in the pub.

We used to fetch water from the village pump. There was one at the end of the council houses – it was lovely water. My father used to go and fetch two big buckets every evening and it was a good time for gossiping.

Betty Dennison (Wicken Bonhunt)

Very Professional

One thing we did look forward to were the concerts, which were held in the Parish Hall, presented by the airmen stationed nearby. They were very entertaining and Frank James, the Irish singer, was very professional.

Margaret Rust (Radwinter)

Girl Guides

I loved the Girl Guides. Dr Hedley Bartlett's daughter, Cynthia, was the captain. I also belonged to the Girls' Friendly Society run by Miss Fisher, and the Missionary Society, also run by Miss Fisher. And I also belonged to the Band of Hope.

Ivy Brown

Sixpenny Hops

We used to have whist drives, occasionally concerts, and we had dancing classes which I used to go to with my mother. We learned to dance to Mr Neale's gramophone.

After I left school I got a bike and I used to cycle into Walden and we used to play darts and visit Sixpenny Hops in the other villages. Later I used to borrow my father's car. I reckoned that if I spent Saturday afternoon cleaning it, I was entitled to have it on Saturday night.

Ron Cain (Wendens Ambo)

Hot Spots

We grew up during the war and the village was very quiet in those days, there were no cars around and, of course, no television. The boys from the RAF camp just outside Radwinter used to put on concerts at the Village Hall and sometimes we had the 'Hot Spots' from Saffron Walden.

Mrs Violet Swan used to run old time dance classes in the village and we had old time dances in the Village Hall.

We had to make our own amusement but I think life was much happier. In those days we had three pubs – the Red Lion, the Plough and the Brewery Tavern, and there was an off-licence in

Maple Lane. There was a little sweet shop opposite the school run by a Mrs Porter.

We used to play football in the meadow, but I was a quiet sort of child and very fond of music – I had an accordion.

Ron Rust (Radwinter)

A Lovely Ride

On Sunday my father and I usually went to see my grandparents at Tindon End. My aunt Elsie, who wasn't married and lived with them, was always waiting to meet us as soon as we came into sight. It was a lovely ride for me because father would take me on his bicycle – no fancy seats then – a cushion would be put over the cross-bar and I just had to hold the handlebars and remember to keep my feet in a certain position. It was lovely, especially going down the hills. We would stay for a while and always be home in time for our Sunday dinner.

Margaret Rust (Radwinter)

CHAPTER 6

Medical matters

Jack Blunt

Everyone in the town knew Dr Justinian Bartlett. He was 'Jack Blunt' – he called a spade a spade. Him and his sisters were lovely doctors. His father was a surgeon. Justinian was a surgeon too.

Jim Surrey

That Little General Hospital

In 1937 Saffron Walden General Hospital was a training hospital. It was very active in those times. All the doctors did their own operations there. There was a nice community spirit. The town was very kind to the hospital, the proceeds of the carnival went to it. We used to have parties and it was the scene of quite a lot of social activity. It certainly was a very good training hospital. We learned far more in that

SAFFRON WALDEN GENERAL HOSPITAL

CENTENARY
1866 — 1966

Saffron Walden General Hospital centenary brochure.

Nursing staff at Saffron Walden General Hospital, late 1930s.

little general hospital than we did at the big hospital in Chelmsford.

Lilian Norman

The Doctors

Dr Hepworth was the senior doctor when I started in the office of the General Hospital in London Road in 1937. After he died, Dr A. Browne from Newport took over. The other doctors were C.A. Weller, J.H. Bartlett, K. Lumsden and A.G. Salaman, and Dr Marjorie Bartlett was the anaesthetist.

All the doctors operated at the hospital – usually three or four tonsils and adenoids most weeks and operations for appendixes etc. They came in every morning to see their patients and were escorted around the wards by matron. Everything was extremely tidy!

Visiting days were Tuesdays, Saturdays and Sundays from two until

four, and no children were allowed to visit! Most of the patients belonged to the contributory scheme and paid 2d a week, so they had free treatment. Others would pay on visiting afternoons perhaps – I think it was about £2 2s 6d a week – or I would send them an account. There was one children's ward and five private patients' single wards, one of which cost seven guineas and the others six.

Pat Witty (Ashdon)

Difficulties

It was extremely difficult to get our mothers into hospital to have their babies, even though there were reasons why they should have been in hospital. We had small premature babies in the district which we just had to rear ourselves.

Then in 1948 the National Health

Domestic staff at Saffron Walden General Hospital, late 1930s.

Service started, but up to then, things were very difficult and we certainly had some extremely small, premature babies and we certainly had some successes!

Nurse Margaret Anderson

Christmas Dinner

We were always invited to a Christmas Dinner in the nurses' dining room for which a goose would be sent over from Ireland because there were several Irish probationers at the Hospital. (They did two years' training at Saffron Walden General and then two years at the Radcliffe Infirmary in Oxford.)

Pat Witty (Ashdon)

Push Bikes

When we first came to Walden in the 1940s we only had bikes – push bikes – and we earned £260 a year! Lots of people thought we had a house free, but we didn't, we had to pay rent. We had to pay 10s a week each for our accommodation, but because it was partly furnished one of us had to pay an extra 2s 6d a week for the furniture. We got by. People were kind to us and you could buy more for your money in those days.

Nurse Margaret Anderson

A Practice in a Country Town

I came to Saffron Walden because I wanted to practise in a country town and there was an opportunity here with Dr Justinian Bartlett. I applied for it and he kindly took me on. This was in 1958.

In those days Saffron Walden was much smaller, the population was about 6,000. Dr Bartlett and his sister were in practice together and I took his sister's place. There were three other practices in the town: Dr Kenneth Lumsden and

Nurse Kathleen Lambert (left) with her sister, Margaret Anderson.

John Cook in Church Street, and George and Gladys Gray in the High Street, and Dr Short whose practice later became Dr Bruet's practice in Park Lane – they went into partnership before she retired.

The practice stretched for a considerable distance. We went out as far as Ickleton to the north, Clavering in the west, Widdington south and Thaxted in the east, covering a much wider area than we did later. We used to have what they called branch surgeries in places like Thaxted, Clavering and Ickleton.

Dr Burton Chalmers

Isolation Hospital

I went to the Isolation Hospital twice, once with measles and later with scarlet fever. It was really very nice; the matron, Mrs Poyser was very, very strict. And I always remember she and her husband had a little green Austin Seven and I can see them now driving up the road in it.

Johnny Porter

Whooping Cough

When we were small all four of us had whooping cough, so we were taken down to the gasworks so that when the coke was taken out of the furnace on big shovels we could inhale

The old Isolation Hospital.

the fumes. The fumes were supposed to clear our lungs. I don't know whether it helped to clear the cough, but we survived!

Margaret McGowan

More Responsibility

By and large the population in those days was much more static, so you got to know the patients better. Later you got an awful lot of new patients coming in and so you didn't get to know them quite as well. In those days you had a good deal more responsibility for the overall care of your patients, because quite a lot of the hospital work was done in Saffron Walden and the majority of women had their babies at home.

Dr Burton Chalmers

Midwifery

Of course in the old days we never knew if we were going to be called out at night. We used to do a lot of midwifery. But gradually more and more mothers went into hospital to have their babies.

Nurse Margaret Anderson

Scarlet Fever

The Isolation Hospital consisted of separate buildings. One building was for scarlet fever and another for diphtheria. I once went to visit somebody and we had to stand outside in the bitter cold and talk to the patients through iron bars. Mrs Poyser was the matron and she was very strict.

Ella Kidman

That Terrible Winter

I remember that terrible winter. It was March 1947 and I was going up Byrds Farm Lane on my bike with all my clobber because a baby was expected and it started to snow, and by the time I got up there I was snowed in, and I had to stay there until the baby was born, which was after midnight. Then the husband and the neighbour next door saw me home through the snow and I had no wellingtons!

Nurse Margaret Anderson

Operating Sessions

We used to take patients' tonsils out at Walden Hospital, and when I first came we had a weekly operating session at the hospital. Dr Bartlett would do the surgery and I did the anaesthetics. It was accepted that you did a lot of the work at the hospital, and we admitted a lot of the patients at the hospital. We had emergency surgery as well – we used to operate on the patients there. We used to do nearly all our own emergency work, set fractures and splints in the hospital. But, if we had a quite serious fracture then the patients had to be sent to Addenbrookes for treatment. But we did a lot of fracture work.

Dr Burton Chalmers

Amputation

During the early part of the century my grandfather attended farms in the district in a pony and trap. On one occasion, it must have been a time close to the First World War, the pony took fright momentarily which resulted in my grandfather sustaining a broken femur. The doctor-surgeon of the day wanted to amputate the leg much to grandfather's annoyance, and he refused to have it done. However, at the hospital before being anaesthetized for the resetting operation he instructed his daughter, Phyllis, to ensure that on no account must his leg be removed. She made sure it wasn't and apart from him suffering arthritic pains later in life, he didn't seem worse for keeping his leg.

Coincidentally many years later - about 1941 – almost to the very day, my father also sustained a fractured femur whilst returning from a night out with the then landlord of the Cross Keys Hotel. The accident happened, I believe, when the landlord's car struck an unlit army vehicle parked during the blackout on the top road between Great and Little Chesterford. He was in hospital the day I left home to go to sea.

Captain C.J. Welch

Removing Teeth

Dr Bartlett used to remove people's teeth in the surgery in the High Street. I would give the anaesthetics. He would take an impression and send it off to the dental laboratory and the laboratory would make the dentures. Mostly it was a case of removing the few remaining teeth the patient had. I don't think the dentists approved.

Dr Burton Chalmers

The double funeral of Alan and Lydia Baynes, both aged 86, March 1914.

Thirty-one Funerals

During the winter of 1946/47 there was this terrible flu epidemic, and I recalled Mr Reg Peasgood telling me that he had had thirty-one funerals during the January. Both my sister and I caught flu and we both had bronchitis, but we were so busy we just had to walk about with it.

Conditions were terrible for the people in the town because we were still on rationing. And all the people in the old houses in Castle Street couldn't get fuel to warm their houses. You see, fuel was rationed and if we had any difficulties with a baby it was absolute murder to try and get enough coal to keep the babies warm. But people were so good to each other. All you'd got to do was to go next door and ask, 'Have you got a bit of coal or whatever?' and you would be given bits here and there to help somebody who had had a baby or was in difficulties. There was a marvellous spirit.

Nurse Margaret Anderson

No Social Life

I was on call all the time, except for Thursday afternoons and alternate Sundays. It was really impossible to take part in the social life of the town. You were tied to the practice all the time. You certainly had no social life at all – it was just part of the job. Nowadays young doctors expect to work more reasonable hours. It is not possible to work the hours we worked when the demand is so heavy. It was not so heavy in those days – you were probably not out visiting all the time.

Dr Burton Chalmers

CHAPTER 7

Wartime

Home-coming party for Hadstock war heroes, April 1946. Jack Crawley is at the extreme left with the open-neck shirt, next is ? Smith and third from left is Reg Wood.

Killed in Action

I lost four brothers in the 1914 war. They were killed in action. Six of us were called up – only two came back. I was in the Royal Naval Air Service. It was considered a gentleman's service and we wore navy blue suits and silk collars.

Ralph Porter

Kindness

I was born in Tottenham and we came to Saffron Walden in 1918. My father was in the army and he was billeted with a Mrs Archer at No. 5 Station Road. My mother wanted to get away from London in wartime and my father asked Mrs Archer if she would take his wife and three children in, until we found somewhere to live. She agreed, which was really very kind of her because she had children of her own.

Ivy Brown

A Bolt from the Blue

The First World War came like a bolt from the blue – like a cloud in the sky. My sister's first husband was killed and my brother, Alan, was killed at about the same time. I was seventeen and I went to work at Salisbury Plain YMCA. My sister went to France as soon as her baby was old enough to leave with my mother; she worked for the French in a casualty clearing station.

The psychological effect of the First

Miss Nancy Tennant.

World War was greater than the second, partly because people were totally unprepared for the First War. We knew the second one was coming and it was just a question of when, and of course it altered social life far more than the First War. After the First World War we still had servants. We had eight before the war. After the second we didn't have any servants – we had a help. Everyone went in the war.

Miss Nancy Tennant (Ugley)

No Heating

During the First War the Boys' British was taken over and we had

97

to have our lessons in Abbey Lane Chapel. There was no heating and we had to stop work occasionally and go for a run round to keep warm.

Stanley Pettit

Flu

My father died a few days before Armistice Day. He had flu and the doctor told him he was fit to go back to the army and he collapsed on Liverpool Street Station. I was six years old at the time and I don't even remember my father.

Ivy Brown

Batmen

When war broke out, at the age of sixteen I joined the Home Guard. I was one of the two youngest in the outfit and we became batmen to the two officers commanding the troop. During harvest time we had to get to work by six-thirty in the morning and we worked until eight o'clock at night, then went on duty with the Home Guard guarding the tunnel at Audley End. When we came off duty it was time to go to work again.

Eddie Clayden (Little Chesterford)

Dad's Army

During the war I was in the Home Guard. We were mainly all farm workers. It was a bit like *Dad's Army* you know! The commanding officers were usually old, retired colonels or other high ranking officers.

Henry Moore (Ashdon)

Ammunition Dump

I remember the ammunition dump at Little Chesterford Park blowing up. It was in May and we were hoeing sugar beet for Mr Fordham. Suddenly we saw four soldiers running towards us. They told us to get into the ditch. We hadn't been there very long before the shells started coming over, then a Nissen hut blew up. We stayed in that ditch for a long time! When we came out we went into the village but there was no one around, but all the doors and windows were open. Mother had left a note saying that they had been evacuated to Great Chesterford. So I took my Home Guard stuff and went to Great Chesterford – because if you lost your uniform and equipment you had to pay for it. Some of the old houses survived the blast better than the new ones.

After that, when we worked on the fields, the soldiers had to accompany us to collect all the ammunition lying around. For a long time we were never allowed to work in the fields without being accompanied by a soldier in case there was any ammunition lying around.

Eddie Clayden (Little Chesterford)

Land Girl

When the Second War started I became a land girl. I worked for

WED.,
MAY 31

Full Moon June 6.
MOONRISE—2.52 p.m.
MOONSET—3.56 a.m.

BLACK-OUT TIMES

LONDON 10.52 p.m. to 5.4 a.m.	**NEWCASTLE** 11.32 p.m. to 4.35 a.m.
BIRMINGHAM 11.3 p.m. to 5.5 a.m.	**GLASGOW** 11.48 p.m. to 4.40 a.m.
BRISTOL 11.1 p.m. to 5.14 a.m.	**PENZANCE** 11.10 p.m. to 5.33 a.m.
LIVERPOOL 11.11 p.m. to 5.8 a.m.	**SOUTHAMPTON** 10.56 p.m. to 5.12 a.m.

Fetter-
Holborn

i - street,
Black-

SIXTY LAY HELPLESS AWAITING EXPLOSION

From Your Own Correspondent

AN ESSEX VILLAGE, Tuesday.

ACROSS a blasted waste of smoking earth, among great oaks torn and shattered, their gaunt branches hanging smashed and splintered, through the forlorn debris and remnants of steel huts, I cautiously picked my way yesterday careful to avoid grenades and shells, mines and ammunition, hot and smoke-blackened, that lay everywhere.

It was in England, on top of a hill in the Home Counties. An expanse of woodland had been gutted by blast and fire. It looked like a shell-torn battlefield.

An ammunition dump hidden in the woods had exploded. A series of explosions followed, destroying the dump.

The loudest explosion was indescribable. It rocked the countryside for miles. It smashed windows in a market town over two miles distant. Seven miles away it threw people off a seat.

Incurables 100 yds. Away

And within a hundred yards of the dump sixty bedridden patients in a home for incurables lay helpless. The explosion smashed their windows, tore down their doors, brought down ceilings, hurled nurses across the wards.

Yet every one of the patients was safely evacuated and taken to neighbouring hospitals. None was seriously injured.

"We were just working away," said Nurse Kathleen Anderson, of the hospital staff, "when we heard what sounded like firing.

"Then we had the warning to evacuate the hospital. That was no sooner said than the explosion came. Windows blew in and the ceilings came down."

Nurse Rosina Leigh, who had been on night duty, was about to leave the hospital when the explosion hurled her against the door.

"It was a good job I was not in bed," she said. "The ceiling came down on some of the beds."

Fifteen American ambulances were quickly on the spot.

"The Americans were really

VILLAGE CLEARED AFTER ARMS DUMP EXPLOSION

wonderful," said Nurse Marie Batchelor. "As I came down with a patient, bricks were falling on my shoulders."

Everything they had was left behind, though Nurse Anderson managed to rescue her engagement ring.

The sentry at a hospital told me two truck loads of casualties had been taken there.

The matron of the local general hospital was unable to give figures but no casualties admitted had been fatal. Some had been able to leave after treatment.

An Army sergeant, picked up bodily and carried eighty yards by the force of blast, was taken straight through an open gateway. He was uninjured.

NFS men, arriving in dozens of tenders were at the flames right of the explosion. as ammunition explo came from thirty mi

They were hampere having to be pumpe. mile from a small brook.

Blast Felt 8 Miles Off

Neighbouring towns and villages up to eight miles distant felt the force of the blast. Two miles from the dump a "Daily Mirror" staff photographer's car was lifted bodily a clear foot from the road.

During the afternoon a warning that there might be gas escaping led to an urgent round-up to see that everybody had a gas mask.

Fortunately the gas danger did not materialise.

By early evening it was decided that the danger of further explosions was over.

Newspaper cutting reporting the blowing up of the ammunition dump at Little Chesterford Park.

Fairycroft House, ARP and ambulance post during the Second World War.

Mr Wedd on his smallholding at Audley End. Then I was called up and I went to work at the Co-op. I also did night duty at the ambulance post in Fairycroft House. We got 2s 6d a night and worked from ten o'clock at night until six in the morning. But I was sleeping at home the night the doodlebug fell. We had decided, my mother and my sister, Ivy, and my younger sister, Dorothy, and myself, all to sleep in the back room which was lucky for us because the doodlebug blew our back door open and the back window and fireplace out in the back bedroom.

I also remember when the ammunition dump blew up at Little Chesterford Park. All the old people who had been evacuated there were brought down to Abbey Lane School and we had to look after them.

Ellen Banks

Top of the House

Dr Hepworth and his wife lived in No. 71 High Street, and I can remember standing right at the top of that house when the ammunition dump blew up at Little Chesterford Park. All the windows in the house rattled.

Nurse Margaret Anderson

Emergencies

During the war I had to ring Old Church Hospital in Romford every morning to give our 'bed states'. That meant I had to say how many beds were available in Saffron Walden General Hospital in case of an emergency.

Pat Witty (Ashdon)

Saffron Walden General Hospital casualty clearing station, during the Second World War. A.R.P. Warden Bert Cornell is the second from right.

Old Bike

My father was head of the A.R.P. for the Saffron Walden District. He had an old bicycle which he had given to him on his twenty-first birthday in 1901, and I remember him pedalling his beat which was from Bridge End to Sparrows End on his old bike. And my mother was billeting officer for Newport and dockers from the East End of London seemed to arrive regularly on our doorstep complaining to mother about the billets their wives were living in. They were huge men, and they called my mother 'love'. No one had ever called my mother 'love' before. No one would have ever dared!

Imogen Mollet (Newport)

Evacuees

In 1939 we were going down to Minehead at the end of August but the holiday was cancelled because all four of us got mumps. So we spent our holiday at our auntie's farm in Debden. We were there until war was declared and then we went home and found two evacuees waiting for us. They soon went home, however; the four children in the family did not take to them very well.

Margaret McGowan

Air Raid Shelters

So much seemed to change so quickly. At school all the windows had white tape put across them – it looked as if

Sainsbury's Maltings at the top of Gold Street, 1940s.

stuff out. It happened in the evening. Some of the lads went on top of the roof with the firemen with their hoses. It was wartime and food was scarce. I remember I dropped a box of butter right down my new suit and it ruined it. The butter was melting in the fire and running down the road. We saved most of it. We saved over ninety per cent of it.

Jim Surrey

The Landmine

Our neighbours, when we lived on Church Hill, were Fred and Joan Goodwin and, at the outbreak of war, my father and Fred Goodwin built an air raid shelter in the garden and lined it with sleepers and put corrugated iron on the top. We used it with Mr and Mrs Goodwin quite often during the air raids. When the landmine fell at Ashdon, Fred was standing in the doorway of the shelter and the landmine fell at Ashdon Halt, the blast threw Fred back into the shelter on top of us and put the hurricane lamp out. But Fred was very concerned about his parents in another part of the village and he walked all the way across the fields to make sure they were all right.

Dorothy Bartlett (Ashdon)

Hand-made Toys

Most of our toys during the war were hand made. I remember I had a Father Christmas, a camel and a golliwog all made by various relatives.

someone had been playing noughts and crosses on them. We had to take our gas masks every day, and woe betide you if you forgot yours!

Then there were the air raid shelters which were built with huge roofs of concrete. Most of the schools had them. Our parents said they were 'nothing but death traps', so some of them dug an earth shelter behind the school.

Margaret Rust (Radwinter)

Fire at the Maltings

I was in the cinema at the time the Maltings caught fire and they made us all get out. I helped to get some of the

Mollie Moore plucking turkeys, 1950s.

My father made us a lovely garage with battery-operated lights. He also made a wooden mechanical digger with moving parts, and a two-funnel liner in the base of which was a mouse trap and if you pushed a button at the bottom the whole thing blew up.

John Maddams

Incendiary Bombs

During the war we had two incendiary bombs in Landscape View just across the road. We were hiding in the house next door – No. 49 – but we would have been much safer in our own house. When we came out of the house all the hedge across the way was on fire. And, of course, a doodlebug was dropped where Tukes Way is now.

Kath Ellis

Searchlights

We went to live at Ricketts farm in the early 1940s. The idea was for us to live there and help run the farm until the time Mr Frederick Furze's eldest son, Jim, came back from the Air Force. Ricketts was a lovely spot, extremely quiet, but after a while the army decided to move the searchlight unit from the Lamb to the meadow in front of Ricketts. Then life began to get hectic. There were about twelve men altogether building the site, and they used to bring their tea, sugar and milk up to the farm for me to make tea for them. When at last they were ready, there was a cookhouse and sleeping quarters as well as the searchlight and big gun. I never did hear that gun go off. I don't think they ever fired it.

Up near the farmhouse they had their R.T. tent where they received messages. When the German planes came across

103

the channel a message was sent – I think from Steeple Bumpstead – we were usually in bed and we would hear the men shouting to each other, and we knew it was time to move. Sometimes we used to go downstairs, and we would look up the beam of the searchlight and see the German planes. The soldiers would try to keep the plane in the beam of the searchlight all the time. As soon as the searchlight went on, the siren would go off in Saffron Walden.

One scene I will never forget is standing right at the top of Ricketts in the stack yard and watching the Battle of Britain when they bombed Debden Aerodrome. It was a lovely sunny day and we stood there watching the planes come down in flames.

Jim Furze never came home to run Ricketts; he was posted missing and soon after, Mr Furze sold the farm.

Mollie Moore (Ashdon)

A.R.P.

When the Second World War came along, I was sent to work on the telephones at the A.R.P. post in Fairycroft. I worked from seven o'clock in the morning until nine o'clock, and from eight o'clock in the evening until ten. For this they payed me 1s 6d an hour!

Marjorie Clark

A Small Attaché Case

My mother was very methodical, and all the insurance policies and important papers were put altogether in a small attaché case, which was always at hand when there was an air raid. Also she had another large case with underclothes and warm garments 'just in case'. We did have some heavy raids. They were always trying for the airfield which surrounded us.

Margaret Rust (Radwinter)

Bombs

Because of the closeness of the railway and the searchlight we had the bombs. Ricketts of course was right near the railway. One night we had several bombs, one hit the railway bridge near to Bartlow and blocked the railway line. The other bombs fell in the fields and made big craters.

When the bombs began to fall we used to go down to the cellar and I used to be terrified in case they hit the farm. I imagined the big house falling on top of us and we would never get out. The frogs and the toads used to make a terrible noise down in the cellar.

Mollie Moore (Ashdon)

Looking After the Horse

When I left school I started work at Gillett's the greengrocers. I started by delivering greengrocery on a bike and then I went on the round at the beginning of the war. We drove a horse and cart, and it was extremely irritating because every time the siren went, you had to take the horse out of the cart and tether it to a lamp-post or somewhere, because if the cart got hit it would have probably turned over and killed the horse. So although the horse was fairly unprotected at least it stood a chance of survival. You had to wait for the all-clear and then get the horse back in the traces.

In those days I think about eighty per cent of the tradespeople used horses and carts. In the end we went over to a car and trailer. I used to go all over the place to the growers, who were supposed to sell all their crops to the jam-makers but were only too happy to let us have stuff from 'under the counter'.

Jim Day

Dancing

I remember people dancing in the Market Place on V.E. Day, and Mr Perry playing his hurdy-gurdy at the bottom of Debden Road and Mrs Rosie Porter offering everyone coming down the road a drink of beer from the crate bought for the occasion.

Daisy Gaze, aged 101

Demobilization

When I came home the lads were having a good time. Some of us had a bit of demob money and we went drinking in the White Horse pub. We used to get a bucket and tell the landlord – Jack Moule – to fill it up, then we'd sit around a table and everyone had to give us a song. If they didn't sing they had to fill the bucket up with beer again. We kept that up for two or three months.

Jim Surrey

Daisy Gaze, aged 101.

105

CHAPTER 8

A changing world

The Hunt in Ashdon Road, 1950s.

Hadstock Band, 1913.

A Forgotten Road

When we first came to Ashdon Road it was quite a forgotten road with lovely open fields all the way round. We would go into the garden and there were sheep on the other side of the hedge. Sometimes the sheep would get into the garden, they would break through the fence. We once had six Highland cattle in the garden in the middle of the night. My uncle helped to build these houses for Isaac Marking Snr; they are about a hundred years old.

Stanley Pettitt

An Orchard and a Chicken Farm

We came to Saffron Walden from Buckinghamshire in 1946, and lived in the first bungalow down on the left in Shepherds Way. It was called The Hut. It was an orchard and a chicken farm. My aunt used to have about a thousand hens at one time. There were no such things as battery hens in those days, and she used to buy in day-old chicks.

Cynthia Wright

Big Families

What I remember most about the village in the old days was that there were so many big families. There

107

Hadstock Band, 1950s.

are a lot of new people in the village now. I used to know everyone, now I don't know half of them. We used to have two shops and two pubs – the Queens Head (now a private house) and the Kings Head. At one time, after work, you could go down to the pub for a game of dominoes and it would be full of local men and they all earned the same money because they all worked on the land. Perhaps those who worked with animals had a little bit more, but everyone was more or less the same. That is the cause of all the trouble these days – money!

Albert Rowlandson (Hadstock)

Two Shops

When I was a lad there were three public houses in the village – The Carpenters Arms, The Falcon and The Queens Head. The Queens Head is the only one left. Where the bungalows are now, it used to be all allotments. We had two shops – both general stores – and a long time ago I believe that part of our house used to be a bakery.

Cyril Perrin (Littlebury)

The Market

I remember Rab Butler speaking in the Market Place and the old market – the cattle market. I remember Saffron Walden market day when it was a proper market. There was the pig market and the cattle market and the general market. And at Watsons the estate agents: in their yard there was all manner of livestock – chickens, ducks, rabbits – it was quite fascinating.

Dr John Eaton

Hadstock Band, 1979.

Traffic

I am the only one living in the village now who has been born in the village. The village was a lot quieter, there was not much going on in Wicken. We usually went into Arkesden or Clavering.

There used to be four farms in the village but they have gradually been bought up by large concerns and have lost their identity. They used to employ several people. We used to have a baker down at the bottom end of the village and the pub was called the Three Horse Shoes, now it's the Coach and Horses.

But the most noticeable change is the traffic - it is non-stop now!

Betty Dennison (Wicken Bonhunt)

The Forge

The George used to be in Gold Street. Where the pillars of the Indian restaurant are there used to be a brick wall. The George was a one-room wide house with a passage. The stables are there still – Dolphin Taxis use them for a garage. The front of that pub was out at the back and there never used to be anything there except a brick wall.

I remember the wooden framed houses which were pulled down to build the Co-op. I helped to build it, the Co-op; I did some of the steelwork.

Between the George and the Forge was an eight-roomed cottage – that is where we lived, and it is still there, but the front of the cottage was pushed back a little. It's now the Oxfam shop.

The Riding stables in the Greyhound Yard, George Street, 1950s.

Joining the shop were about three stables belonging to the Greyhound. And the foundation of that was a six-foot wall and a pair of double cottages which shut off the Greyhound. The Greyhound yard was a cobblestone yard and the opposite side of the yard there used to be a trough about six feet long with a pump which pumped water for the horses to drink from a well. It was more of a relic than useful. The front of the Greyhound faced the High Street – it's now Dollond & Aitchison and the *Weekly News* office.

Hubert Bell

Condemned

Before the war a lot of the cottages were condemned and then the war came along and people who had been evacuated needed somewhere to live; and after the war there was a shortage of houses and people started to modernize the old cottages – and so they were saved.

Irene Hudgell (Arkesden)

Prickly Bushes

I remember when they had cricket on the common. During the winter months they always fenced it off with dead, prickly bushes, about five or six feet high, to keep the boys from the

110

pitch. I used to enjoy watching the cricket on the common. It was lovely on Saturday afternoon. Lots of people would enjoy watching it and they would come around with the collecting box.

Stanley Pettitt

Commuting Village

The most significant change in the village is that all the old village people have gone. There are a lot of people in Arkesden I still don't know –

A quiet lane in Arkesden, 1940s.

Fred and Isobel Furze with three of their four children. Their eldest son Jim, killed during the Second World War, is at the extreme right, Bob is holding his mother's hand and Pat is leaning against Jim.

people come and go. It is now more of a commuting village. It used to be an agricultural village but not any more. There is only one farm in the village now and that is run by the farmer, his son and one employee. When I was a child the men used to walk from Clavering to Chardwell Farm, I think they must have employed five or six men.

Irene Hudgell (Arkesden)

All Horses

My grandfather, Luke James Furze, bought Goldstones for my father, Frederick Furze, in 1911. In those days

111

Saffron Walden Cattle and Poultry Markets, 1940s.

it was a mixed farm – and still is. It was 336 acres which was quite big because there were a lot of small farms in Essex in those days. At that time it was all horses. My father would have had about ten men working for him, including a shepherd, horsemen and stockmen. We also had some poultry but my mother did not look after them, although she did help to pack eggs for market. She also made butter and lovely Devonshire cream. I think my parents would have been more or less self-supporting.

They would go into Walden by pony and trap, probably the only time the front door of the farmhouse was used – now everyone drives up to the back door in their cars!

As the years went by my father bought up various farms as they became available. It was extremely difficult for the small farms to keep going. Now we

have 690 acres.

My parents had four children: Betty and Pat, my two sisters, and my brother Jim and me. One of the farms my father bought was Ricketts. He bought it for my brother Jim in 1937. The land was almost derelict but we brought it round. But Jim was a pilot in the war and he was reported missing, presumed killed, during the Battle of Britain.

Bob Furze (Ashdon)

Happy Days

It used to be very difficult. We used to live off £3 or £4 a week. I never remember giving Lilian more than £5 or £6 week, and we had four children to support. We look back on those days as very happy days though. We always had

112

The Paddling Pool in Debden Road, later filled in to make way for houses.   Councillor Bob Eastham is paddling.

a week's holiday every year. The town was more of a community then. We always seemed to be doing something.

Arthur Norman

The Smell of Malt

Years ago when I was a little boy I always remember there was always the smell of malt. We had so many maltings in the town. The smell of roasting malt was all over the town. It smelled good and it was good. Perhaps things were a bit rougher. We had a market with cattle, pigs and sheep. And the poultry market where people sold produce. They used to sell butter there. You could get two pounds of butter for a shilling. Everyone had an allotment and they used to put a lot of vegetables in the market – those that Mr Gillett didn't buy.

Jim Surrey

Living in a Field

Living in Landscape View was just like living in a field. I often used to say that I would prefer to live in the middle of the fen at Swaffham Prior. I had a young baby in a pram, and although the baker and the butcher delivered, most things had to be fetched from town and that meant a long walk, pushing the baby in the pram all the way.

Seven acres of greenhouses with Engelmann's Nurseries, Ashdon Road in the middle distance.

No one wanted to come and live in Landscape View – people in the town used to called it Africa! I remember the waterworks across the way being built. My two boys used to play in the fields nearby. And then they made the paddling pool and we would have a lovely time over there. People would walk up from the town with the children and bring a picnic with them and spend all day by the paddling pool in summer.

Marjorie Clark

No Sanitation

When we first came to Ashdon in 1940 many of the houses had no sanitation. There was some electricity but a lot of the houses still had paraffin lamps. When we were first married in 1954 we lived in a house which was one of a pair of cottages on the Bartlow Road. We got our water from a well in the garden and we had to turn the handle forty times to fetch up one bucketful of water. My wife had to do the washing in the copper out in the wash house at the back. We had to fill the copper by hand and light the fire under it and boil the water that way.

Dennis Bartlett (Ashdon)

Blackberrying

When we first came to Pleasant Valley there was only this row of houses. There were no houses opposite up to Newport Road and up to the end and at the back of the Isolation Hospital, it was all fields. We were right out in the country and it was lovely. There were just one or two cottages down Hilltop Lane and there was the Isolation Hospital. The rest was all open fields with the plantation on the corner which was beautiful. We would play there and pick violets in the spring. We would walk across the meadows blackberrying. Mr Britton, the butcher, would graze his cattle where Landscape View is now.

Ellen Banks

Saffron Walden High Street, 1940s.

Perfect

I have seen a lot of changes in the town. The main thing is the trade, the shops and where people lived. Up to the beginning of the war no one ever moved house unless the rent was twopence cheaper next door. The population was reasonable, it stayed at 6,000 until we got pestered with the evacuees. It was just perfect and then they started changing it.

Jim Day

Spriggs

My father, William Charles Mallett, bought the farm in 1942. It was a small mixed farm, terribly run down. A typical small, Essex farm. There was no electricity. No anything. There was a pond under one of the floors. The yard wasn't concreted and if it was raining it was awash with mud. There were twelve acres of orchard, but apart from that, we grew all the crops – wheat, oats, potatoes, mangels and hay. We used to have the threshing tackle up here every year. Mr Fordham from Bendysh Hall used to come round all the farms with his big threshing machine.

I decided that we couldn't possibly have a big enough farm to grow corn and thought we would concentrate on the thing that I really liked and that was growing fruit. We decided we would put the whole farm down to fruit.

Bill Mallett (Ashdon)

115

Tom Dewing, aged 101.

Ashdon Road

We had Engelmann's greenhouses out at the back. We never thought we would see the day when Engelmann's would close. There were no council houses in Ashdon Road, it was beautiful, the birds used to sing and the cuckoo was in the fields. People used to walk along the road and pick white violets in the springtime. There were no houses after the Grammar School. Provident House was Engelmann's house. Now they have made it into flats.

Mrs Hannah Wells

A Quiet Market Town

When we came to Saffron Walden in 1931 it was a quiet market town with a population of about 6,000. Today the population is about 13,000 and many changes have taken place. It was then the Borough of Saffron Walden with a Mayor and Corporation.

At that time there was a wide variety of shops catering for the normal needs of the townsfolk and the people living in the villages around. Almost all those businesses were privately run and had been in the family for two or three generations. In many cases the shopkeeper and his family lived above the shop. Over the years many businesses have changed hands and several are now branches of larger associations, and in recent years a number of small businesses have closed down being unable to compete with the supermarket which now occupies part of the old Pig Market.

Tom Dewing, aged 101

So Much To Do

There was so much to do. We waited and waited for the electricity and we were so excited when it finally came, and the first time we switched on there was a blaze of light for precisely five minutes and then there was a major breakdown and we had no electricity for the next two days. Fuses had blown everywhere.

There was no sanitation either – just a well and a pump. All mod cons came gradually. We got mains water shortly after moving in – in 1946 – because the

Outside The Fox, Radwinter Road, Ashdon. Carry Cornell is standing in the doorway.

mains was at the gate. All the water was pumped from the well at the gate up into a tank which fed the tap in the house.

It was a tremendous job keeping the wicks of the oil lamps trimmed, but they were so warming, comforting and lovely. They gave a beautiful soft light, but of course they needed an awful lot of work. And of course we had no detergents in those days, washing soda was all we had to soften the water and help keep us clean. We used to boil loads of water in a copper to scald the milk pans. It just became a complete way of life – it was what we had to do.

Pat Mallett (Ashdon)

The Fly

Grandmother used to visit us at Christmas time and for special occasions. She would hire the Rose and Crown 'fly' – better known as a cab – which was really a box on wheels. There was a step at the back, and as children we would run behind the cab and jump on the step. Latterly it was driven by a man named Mr Sims. He was the licensee of the Tap which was a pub in the Rose and Crown Yard. It is still there: walk through and on the right hand side – Barclays Bank side – the brick building is still to be seen. It used to cost 1s 6d to fetch grandmother. That was when she was in her eighties or nineties.

Richard Faircloth

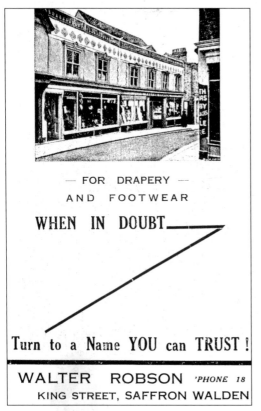

— FOR DRAPERY —
AND FOOTWEAR

WHEN IN DOUBT

Turn to a Name YOU can TRUST !

WALTER ROBSON 'PHONE 18
KING STREET, SAFFRON WALDEN

Advert for Robsons, 1933. Note the telephone number, 18!

All Mates

The village is not the same as it was when I was young. You see, you don't know half the people – they come and go. The pubs have all gone, except the Rose and Crown. We always used to go to the Bricklayers Arms – we were all mates there.

There used to be two bakers' shops in the village, one where the Labour Hall is now and one which is now a house called Thatchings. There were two grocers' shops, one near the Baptist Chapel and two blacksmiths and an undertaker. One blacksmith's shop was in front of the garage and there was another in Radwinter Road near Kates

Lane. There used to be an old man who made shoes. He could soon make you a pair of hobnail boots. He used to live where the old Post Office was in Radwinter Road.

Fred Goodwin (Ashdon)

Miss Gibson

When we came here Miss Gibson lived at the top of the High Street. She lived in that big house (Hill House) with one servant. Every Empire Day she used to supply the Boys' British School with buns. And I can remember her dying, and the Gibson Estate with its garden and meadow being sold. Behind the garden there was a meadow with cows in it. The gardener used to live in a little house at the top of the High Street. I remember him taking us round and showing us the chrysanthemums.

Tom Dewing, aged 101

Not the same

The town is not the same. It used to be such a nice little town. We knew everybody, we still know quite a few people but there are a lot of strangers. In those days we had the railway.

Doris Shepherd

A train standing in Saffron Walden station, 1940s or 1950s.

Beautiful Coffee

I used to enjoy walking down Fairycroft. There was Mr Cooper's music shop on the corner, and next door a draper's shop and then down at the bottom there was a rag and bone shop where, if you had a rabbit skin, they would give you 10d for it. You could go into the Co-op in the High Street and Mrs Peters would make you a beautiful cup of coffee for 6d. And opposite Woolworths was another nice grocer's shop – I think it was called Cro's Stores.

I don't think much of Saffron Walden now. I think it has been spoiled. They have ruined it! All the lovely little shops have gone.

Daisy Gaze, aged 101

The Unemployment Problem

The Cement Cottages, sometimes called the 'Mud Houses' were built by Mr Bell sometime in 1908/9. They dug the ballast out of the gardens at the back. Gibsons had them built for the relief of the unemployed. They built three lots of cottages – Springfield Cottages in Thaxted Road, Westfields and those. All done to relieve the unemployment problem. There was a lot of development of the town up to the First World War and then it stopped. The timber yard at the corner of Victoria Avenue was intended as a Lay Church for the Church of England.

Richard Faircloth

Cro's Stores, Saffron Walden High Street, 1940s.

The First Shop

The first shop I ever went into in Saffron Walden was the International Stores in King Street, and I stayed with them until they closed – sixty-four years at the same shop! But in those days they did deliver the groceries, and when we first moved here they were delivered by horse-drawn van driven by a man called Mr Flack. Later, of course, they changed to a motor van, and then sometime in the 1970s they stopped delivering altogether.

Marjorie Clark

Five Pubs

My father was the village cobbler. He had a little cottage near the garage, then later, a small hut at the top of Rectory Lane. In those days there were five pubs in the village. Even the Conservative Club was a pub at one time – it was called the White Horse. The Brewery used to bring barrels of drinking water for the Lamb. They had a well, but I think it must have got contaminated. The Bonnet at Stevington End used to do a marvellous trade. It used to be so crowded you could hardly move. But the Rose and Crown has not changed quite so much since my young days.

George Ford (Ashdon)

A Terrible Street

Castle Street was a terrible street. They were always fighting. It was

Castle Street fifty years ago.

the slum of Walden. There were rows of little houses but a lot of them have been pulled down now. Everyone who lived in Castle Street seemed to drink a lot. There were quite a few pubs. It seems funny to think where they got the money from. It has changed a lot down there. We used to get fish and chips from Elsom's and there was a laundry there too, but it has gone now.

Mollie Moore (Ashdon)

Spotless

Stanley was born in Castle Street in Middle Square. It was only a two up, two down but my mother-in-law kept the house spotless. She brought up four sons and one daughter in that house. You could always guarantee a fight down Castle Street every Saturday night.

Joan Butcher

A Happy Little Road

Basil came home in 1945 and we were married in 1948. He got this job as gardener at the Friends' School and the house, No. 7 Westfields, went with the job. All the houses were privately owned except ours which was owned by the school. They were built by the Gibson family for their employees. We had no hot water, only a copper and a tin bath in front of the fire. The toilet was outside round the corner, and the children used to go out with candles. It was a very happy little road with a real neighbourhood feeling. I knew most of the people who lived in them. We were there over thirty-seven years.

Joy Waterman

121

Insecurity

I don't think the village was happier in those days. Life was hard and women grew old before their time. I think it was the insecurity. If your husband fell ill there was nothing coming in at all. I remember old Mrs Townsend: she had a family of ten and her husband earned 12s a week. She used to say, 'There weren't never enough to go round, Miss!' The thing they didn't suffer from which people do now is loneliness – that is the great change.

Miss Nancy Tennant (Ugley)

The Hedge

My parents had this house built in 1902. I was only two years old at the time. When we first came here there was a hedge across the road – about six doors down – the road ended there and the remains of the hedge can still be seen. Then they cut it down and carried the road through right to the bottom corner and out into Thaxted Road. Then they built the Mud Houses. We used to watch the men making the blocks of cement and as they made them they put them up. The cement blocks, which are hollow in the middle, were made on the spot. Those in Victoria Gardens were built in 1901, so those in Victoria Avenue must have been built about 1908.

In those days the road was made up but not the pavements. Where the bungalows are now, there was a timber yard – Bell's. All the logs were brought in on a horse-drawn dray and they used to pile these logs up. They used to have shire horses with a long chain, and then drive the horses across the road until they had several logs on top of each other.

We used to get into trouble when we used to squeeze through a gap in the railings and play on the logs. Bell's developed most of Victoria Avenue.

Cyril Shepherd

Sandwiches

When the children were home during the summer holidays, I would make them up each a packet of sandwiches and off they would go for the whole day to play up near the Battle Ditches. Children couldn't do that now, it wouldn't be safe.

Rosie Porter

Opportunity to Buy

I found the villagers very friendly and I was soon accepted. But village life began to change for this reason. Some of the houses belonged to Mr Brocklebank who was a wealthy man, and he decided to sell the estate, and he gave all his tenants the opportunity of buying their houses. They bought them for about £50, with the result that quite a few people bought their cottages in the early 1920s. Well, after a few years some of the old people died and the houses were sold and there was a developer called Mr Myers who came around and bought these old cottages and modernized them. Mains water came to Hadstock in 1933, so he put

The Bell, Wendens Ambo, c. 1900.

bathrooms in and septic tanks so that they had flush toilets, with the result that you had people coming in from outside which the locals referred to as foreigners – ex-majors, civil servants, everyone in the middle class – and the villagers resented them. From the 1930s until the beginning of the war the foreigners gradually took the village over and did quite a lot of good for the village, but at first they were resented.

Reg Wood (Hadstock)

Flooded

In wintertime Duck Street and West End were very often flooded and we would wait for Harry White, who lived at the Water Mill in Mill Lane, to open the flood gates and then the water would go down very quickly, but by that time the damage had already been done. This was before they built Holland's Mill. It was a flour mill and it was water driven.

Ron Cain (Wendens Ambo)

Cinder Path

Butler Close was just a cinder path down to the railway line. They used to bring the wagons loaded with coal to the bottom of the cinder path and Mr Housden would come with his horse and cart and load the coal onto the cart to take it to the gas works in Thaxted Road.

Where the new houses are now in Victoria Avenue was an Esso Petroleum depot. Again, the Esso petrol was brought by rail and off-loaded into the storage tanks, then delivered to the surrounding farms for their tractors. Tommy Weston was in charge of it for many years.

Hazel Martin

The Prairie

Butlers Close was called Faircloth's field. Another name for it was The Prairie. It was very rural in those days. We were right on to Thaxted Road where there were no houses at all at one time. We could go for a walk in the open country.

Doris Shepherd

Nothing but Fields

Father built No. 25 about 1902. It was the first house to be built in Victoria Avenue. Then they moved to No. 27. It was built entirely to mother's specification. We had oil lamps and there was no sewerage and the septic tanks were emptied by the night soil cart because there was no drainage. We had a bath but, of course, it could not be plumbed in. Later we had the town gas.

It was a mud road in those days, and all the water drained from the top of the road downwards, eventually finding its way into the Slade. In those days there was nothing but fields. We were living in the country and there were small farms all around us.

Richard Faircloth

Steam and Sparks

Taylors from Littlebury had a chaff factory and bought all the chaff from the local farms - and during the evenings their traction engines and trailers loaded with chaff would come down Wenden Hill belching steam and sparks. It was always a danger to thatched cottages. Drage and Kent had Foden steam wagons – they came from Chrishall and they carted granite from Audley End station. They used to fill up their engines at the brook near our cottage.

Holland's Mill was in full swing in those days too. It had a 90 ft chimney shaft built with red brick carried by my father by horse and cart from the brick works at Mill Lane.

Ron Cain (Wendens Ambo)

Horse-drawn Traffic

When I first came to Debden Road all the traffic was horse-drawn, and there wasn't nearly so much of it. You could get everything you needed from the shops nearby, there was no need to go into town. The butcher's was where Osborne's the electrical shop is now, and next door was the grocer's. Across the way in London Road was a small general stores run by a lady called Miss Golden.

Rosie Porter

The church, Wendens Ambo, 1900.

All Gone

At the top of the High Street there was a cinema which was demolished to make way for a block of flats called The Maltings.

For shopping we had the International Stores, the Home & Colonial and the Co-op where they would pack butter whilst you waited. We didn't have a Woolworths in those days. We had Street's the Drapers in the High Street and Mr Spurge in King Street, Hardwick's the fishmongers and – of course – Penning's the grocers. They have all gone now.

Ivy Brown

Dog Cart

My father always went to Stansted Station in the dog cart. He had more faith in that than his car.

Gradually he learned to drive in a rather terrifying manner. Mother was very good at driving, she drove a pair of horses. My sister had a pony and cart all during the war.

Miss Nancy Tennant (Ugley)

Transport

When we walked to school we would meet several harmless tramps walking from Saffron Walden Union to Royston Institution. They would call at the cottages to collect water for making tea – if they were lucky they would be given the tea. We used to be passed by Miss Prime on her new Hudson two-stroke motor cycle coming from Duddenhoe End to the Bank where she worked in Saffron Walden. And Bill Ruck who ran motor car hire from Chrishall, also his daughter Dorothy and Mr Crocker in

The cinema at the top of the High Street, 1935.

his model T Ford charabanc. And the vicar of Langley used to pass us on his Triumph motor cycle.

Teddy Flack from Elmdon – he ran the Carrier public house, now a private house – he had a horse and trap and he was hired to take people to Audley End station. He was extremely deaf, but it didn't matter because there was not much traffic on the roads in those days. Mr Gibbs from the Axe and Compasses at Arkesden had a Model T Ford and he was used to take people to Audley End and Saffron Walden. This would be about 1922.

My mother used to cycle into Saffron Walden on Fridays. She used to keep poultry and take the eggs to Walden to sell.

Ron Cain (Wendens Ambo)

Only the Rich

When Mr Pateman the butcher was ill, they laid straw on the road to deaden the noise of the old carts and wagons as they rattled by. This was some-thing only the rich people could do, the poor had to put up with the noise.

Ralph Porter

Self-Supporting

In those days Radwinter was very self-supporting. We had a coal merchant and a post office. The Brewery Tavern brewed beer, sold clothes and had a butcher's shop – they sold almost everything!

Ron Rust (Radwinter)

Prince's Well, Radwinter, c. 1900.

Sun Petrol

Sampford has changed since I was a boy. There was only one person who went out of the village to work and that was Mr Miller at Tewes Manor. He used to travel up to London daily. All the others worked on the land. Today I can't think of anyone, apart from the farmers themselves, who works on the land. Most of the people are commuters and retired people.

There used to be three shops, three pubs – the White Horse, the Black Bull and the Red Lion, two shoemakers, a blacksmith, and a coal merchant who also sold petrol in a can at 10d a gallon. It was called Sun Petrol and it wasn't much good. There was also a chimney sweep called 'Shine Wright'.

Bill Reader (Great Sampford)

Footsteps

Times have changed. There used to be twenty-six men working at Radwinter Hall and we knew them all by their footsteps as they passed by on their way to work. Now the farm no longer functions – it has been turned over to 'set aside'.

Joyce Jarvis (Radwinter)

Terrible Poverty

The first thing we did was to go round to every single house in the village. There was terrible poverty. People could be turned out of their house if their husband got ill. There was no backup of any kind. People were really hungry – no school meals. We had to provide all kinds of things like

127

The White Horse, Great Sampford, 1920s.

bed-pans, buckets and kettles.

Then we organized the dust cart. Up until then there was no refuse collection in Ugley. We got someone to allow us to dump rubbish and we paid 6d a week for a horse and cart. The horse was very restive and we had to rush out to get the rubbish into the cart.

No-one had water or electric light. People just had wells. The husband filled two buckets before he went to work. I don't think the village had water until after the Second War. When water finally came, a charming woman of the village asked me to come and admire her stand pipe. When I said how useful it would be, she said she wouldn't use it, she preferred the well! When we had electricity I went to congratulate one family and the husband said, 'But you can't turn it down!' It is interesting when one has been in the same place all the time, being able to observe all the changes.

Miss Nancy Tennant (Ugley)

Bond Street

Debden Road was known as Bond Street years ago. I don't know why. At one time there was quite a feud between the people of Debden Road and the people of Castle Street. I don't know how it started, but if a man from Castle Street came into Debden Road there was always a fight and the same thing happened if a man from Debden Road strayed into Castle Street.

Ralph Porter